D0832339

TS

Why Aeschylus in an Hour?   v
by Carl R. Mueller

Introduction   vii
by Robert Brustein

Aeschylus: IN A MINUTE   ix

Aeschylus: HIS WORKS   x

ONSTAGE WITH AESCHYLUS: Introducing
Colleagues and Contemporaries of Aeschylus   xiii

AESCHYLUS: In an Hour   **1**

APPENDICES

Dramatic Moments from the Major Plays   41

Aeschylus: THE READING ROOM   76

Awards: "And the winner is . . ."   85

INDEX   86

Why Playwrights in an Hour?

This new series by Smith and Kraus Publishers titled Playwrights in an Hour has a dual purpose for being: one academic, the other general. For the general reader, this volume, as well as the many others in the series, offers in compact form the information needed for a basic understanding and appreciation of the works of each volume's featured playwright. Which is not to say that there don't exist volumes on end devoted to each playwright under consideration. But inasmuch as few are blessed with enough time to read the splendid scholarship that is available, a brief, highly focused accounting of the playwright's life and work is in order. The central feature of the series, a thirty- to forty-page essay, integrates the playwright into the context of his or her time and place. The volumes, though written to high standards of academic integrity, are accessible in style and approach to the general reader as well as to the student and, of course, to the theater professional and theatergoer. These books will serve for the brushing up of one's knowledge of a playwright's career, to the benefit of theater work or theatergoing. The Playwrights in an Hour series represents all periods of Western theater: Aeschylus to Shakespeare to Wedekind to Ibsen to Williams to Beckett, and on to the great contemporary playwrights who continue to offer joy and enlightenment to a grateful world.

Carl R. Mueller
School of Theater, Film and Television
Department of Theater
University of California, Los Angeles

Introduction

Aeschylus is the first Western playwright whose work has come down to us in more than fragments. He began writing tragedy 2,500 years ago, just a year after the beginning of the fifth century BCE. Of his seventy or more plays, only seven survive in relatively complete form. Yet, this remote Athenian giant has continued to remain one of the most powerful and influential playwrights who ever lived.

Aeschylus' plays — like those of his contemporaries and followers — are all based on Homeric myths. In this, Greek tragedy most resembles the Christian mystery plays that were also dependent on sacred stories (the mystery plays started with the Creation and ended with the Harrowing of Hell). But the more sophisticated European drama that followed the mystery plays mostly rejected Biblical material, finding inspiration in secular stories. The body of Greek tragedy, on the other hand, never abandoned its hieratic roots. It formed a continuing series of variations on the same myths seen from different points of view — as for example, the way that Aeschylus, Sophocles, and Euripides each handled the recognition scene between Electra and Orestes.

The one trilogy Aeschylus wrote — indeed the only extant Greek trilogy (though it lacks a requisite satyr play) — is his *Oresteia*. All of the playwright's strengths are evident in these plays — his pious, dense, obscure style; his patriotic passion for his country and his interest in its growing legal system; his sense that humans are subject to celestial oversight. In the scope and ambition of his work, Aeschylus will not only influence his Greek successors but he will function as a model for the drama to come, especially in nineteenth-century Germany and twentieth-century Europe and America.

Eugene O'Neill's monumental trilogy *Mourning Becomes Electra,* for example, owes a huge debt to the *Oresteia,* as does Jean-Paul Sartre's *Les Mouches (The Flies),* and T. S. Eliot's *The Family Reunion.* Although Western dramatists still remain reluctant to turn over Biblical soil, they have shown no hesitation in tilling the Homeric myths of Greek drama. And it is Aeschylus, rather than the more modern Sophocles or skeptical Euripides, who has remained their primary model, adapted for modern purposes. In 1966, for example, Robert Lowell wrote a version of Aeschylus' *Prometheus Bound* that served as a fierce condemnation of the Vietnam War.

The reason for Aeschylus' continuing influence on modern drama, I believe, is his passionate concern for the Greek city-state where he lived and his dedicated patriotic fervor. He wrote *The Persians* after having actually participated in the Persian Wars. He designed *Seven Against Thebes* as a fierce condemnation of civil strife. He conceived *The Suppliants* as a plea for women in choosing their own mates. And in the last play of his *Oresteia,* namely *The Eumenides,* he fashioned a theatrical metaphor for the founding of the Athenian justice system. In this play, pursued by the Furies, Orestes is brought before the Court of the Areopagus for the murder of his mother. And when Athena chooses to resolve human conflict through law rather than tribal revenge, he is arraigned, in the first trial in history, before a jury of his peers. Typically, the jury is hung, and Athena casts the deciding vote for Orestes on the premise that the mother is not the true parent of the child.

Although properly outraged by this decision, the Furies are finally persuaded by Athena to transform into the more benign Eumenides, and let the courts rather than tribal vengeance decide on future criminal issues. As an isolated legal decision, Athena's patriarchal prejudices are hardly designed to endear her to modern readers. But the scene represents a major step in the progress of civilization, the creation of an organized legal system within a tragic play. Aeschylus emerges from the *Oresteia,* as he does from his other six extant works, not only as a great poet and dramatist but also as a great patriot, as a great peacemaker, as a great civic philosopher.

Robert Brustein
Founding Director of the Yale and American Repertory Theatres
Distinguishing Scholar in Residence, Suffolk University

Aeschylus

IN A MINUTE

AGE YEAR (BCE)

AGE	YEAR (BCE)	
—	525	**Enter Aeschylus.**
4	521	Buddha leaves home to devote his life to philosophy and asceticism.
10	515	Construction is completed on Temple in Jerusalem.
15	510	The Roman Republic is established.
25	500	Babylonian astronomer Naburiannu determines length of lunar month.
26	**499**	**Aeschylus' first tragic play (unknown) premieres in Athens at the City Dionysia.**
27	498	Alexander I takes the reigns from his father as king of Macedon.
28	497	Potidaea is saved from Persian rule by the first recorded tsunami in history.
31	494	Persia annihilates the Greek cit, Miletos.
35	**490**	**The Greeks, Aeschylus among them, overwhelm the Persians at Marathon.**
38	487	Comedy debuts on the ancient Greek stage at the City Dionysia.
39	486	First Buddhist Council is established at Rejgaha.
40	485	Xerxes I becomes king of Persia.
41	**484**	**Aeschylus wins first dramatic contest in Athens.**
42	483	Themistocles builds a navy, founding Athenian sea power.
46	479	Confucius, the Chinese philosopher, dies.
47	478	The marble temple to Apollo at Delphi is built.
49	476	Phyrnichus — *Phoenician Women*
50	475	Phyrnichus — *Phoenissae*
53	**472**	**Aeschylus — *Persians***
54	471	Plebeians in Rome choose their own tribunal.
55	470	The great Greek philosopher Socrates is born.
57	**468**	**Sophocles introduces a third actor and defeats Aeschylus for first prize in tragedy.**
58	**467**	**Aeschylus — *Seven Against Thebes***
60	465	A series of earthquakes shake Sparta to the core.
63	462	Pericles' rise to power in Athens begins.
66	**459**	**Aeschylus — *Suppliant Women***
67	**458**	**Aeschylus — *Oresteia***
69	**456**	**Aeschylus — *Prometheus Bound***
69	**456**	**Exit Aeschylus.**

In one minute or less, this section gives you a snapshot of the playwright's world. From historical events to the literary landscape of the time, this brief list catalogues events that directly or indirectly impacted the playwright's writing.

ix

Aeschylus

HIS WORKS

[Wrote 78 plays we know of, 7 of which are existing]
[CAPITALS = existing plays]

DRAMATIC WORKS

Dates Known

AGAMEMNON 458
EUMENIDES 458
LIBATION BEARERS 458
PERSIANS 472
PROMETHEUS BOUND 456
SEVEN AGAINST THEBES 467
SUPPLIANTS 463

Dates Unknown

Aitna
Amymone
Archer Nymphs
Argo
Atalanta
Athamas
Award of Arms
Bassarids
Bone Gatherers
Cabiri
Callisto
Cercyon

This section presents a complete list of the playwright's known works.

Chamber Makers

Children of Heracles

Circe

Danaids

Daughters of the Sun

Edonians

Egyptians

Eleusinians

Epigoni

Escort

Europa

Ghost Raiders

Glaucus of Potniai

Glaucus the Seagod

Heralds

Hypsipyle

Iphigenia

Ixion

Cretan Women

Laius

Lemnian Women

Lion

Lycurgus

Memnon

Myrmidons

Mysians

Nemea

Nereids

Netfishers

Niobe

Nurses of Dionysus

Oedipus

Oreithyia

Palamedes

Penelope

Pentheus

Perrhaibian Women

Pgorcides

Philoctetes

Phineus

Phrygians

Phrygian Women

Polydeuces

Priestesses

Prometheus the Fire Bearer

Prometheus the Fire Kindler

Prometheus Unbound

Semele

Sisyphus the Runaway

Sisyphus the Stone Roller

Sphinx

Telephus

Thracian Women

Visitors to the Isthmus

Weighing of Souls

Women of Argos

Women of Salamis

Wool Carders

Young Men

Onstage with Aeschylus

*Introducing Colleagues and
Contemporaries of Aeschylus*

 ## THEATER

Aristophanes, Athenian comic playwright [ca. 448–380]

Crates, Athenian Old Comedy playwright [ca. mid-5th century]

Cratinus, Athenian Old Comedy playwright [ca. 520–423]

Epicharmus, Sicilian Greek comic poet, [ca. 540–450]

Euripides, Athenian tragic playwright [ca. 480–406]

Phrynichus, Greek tragic playwright [ca. 511–476]

Pratinas, introduced satyr play to Athens [ca. late 6th–early
5th century]

Sophocles, Athenian tragic playwright [ca. 496–406]

Sophron, Syracusan writer of mimes [ca. 5th century]

Thespis, Greek actor and playwright [ca. 6th century]

 ## ARTS

Micon, Greek painter [ca. mid-5th century]

Phidias, Greek sculptor [ca. 480–ca. 430]

Polygnotus, Greek painter [ca. 500–440]

Pythagoras, Greek music theorist [ca. 570–ca. 495]

 ## POLITICS/MILITARY

Aristides, founded Delian League [ca. 530–468]

Artaxerxes, king of Persia [ca. 5th century]

Cimon of Athens, Athenian statesman [ca. 510–450]

This section lists contemporaries whom the playwright may or may not have known. Since fewer notables are known from
the Classical Period, we have included some who predated the playwright.

Cyrus the Younger, Persian prince and general [ca. 5th century]
Darius I, king of Persia [ca. 549–486]
Darius II, king of Persia [ca. 5th century–404]
Herodotus, Greek historian [ca. 484–ca. 425]
Mardonius, Persian military commander [ca. 5th century–479]
Nicias, Athenian statesman and general [ca. 469–413]
Pericles, Athenian statesman and general [ca. 495–429]
Pisistratus, Athenian tyrant, [ca. 6th century–527]
Themistocles, Athenian statesman and general [ca. 524–459]
Xerxes I, king of Persia [ca. 520–465]
Xerxes II, king of Persia [ca. 5th century]

SCIENCE

Alcmaeon of Croton, natural philosopher [ca. 6th century]
Ictinus, designed rebuilding of the Athenian Acropolis
     [ca. mid-5th century]
Callicrates, designed rebuilding of the Athenian Acropolis
     [ca. mid-5th century]
Protagoras, Greek mathematician and philosopher [ca.
     490–420]
Susrata, Indian surgeon [ca. 6th century]

LITERATURE

Aesop, Greek fable writer, [ca. 620–560]
Anacreon, Greek poet [ca. 570–ca. 488]
Bacchylides, Greek poet [ca. 507–ca. 450]
Pindar, Greek composer and poet [ca. 522–443]
Simonides of Ceos, Greek poet [ca. 556–468]

RELIGION/PHILOSOPHY

Anaxagoras, Greek philosopher from Asia Minor [ca. 500–428]
Confucius, Chinese philosopher [ca. 551–479]

Empedocles, Greek philosopher [ca. 490–430]

Ezra, Hebrew scribe [ca. 5th century]

Heraclitus, Greek philosopher [ca. 535–475]

Meh-Ti, Chinese philosopher [ca. 5th century]

Mo-tzu, Chinese philosopher [ca. 470–391]

Parmenides, Greek philosopher [ca. early 5th century]

Siddhartha Gautama, the Buddha, founder of Buddhism
    [ca. 563–483]

Socrates, Greek philosopher [ca. 470–399]

Xenophanes, Greek philosopher [ca. 570–480]

AESCHYLUS

in an
hour

BEGINNINGS

We know so little about the life of Aeschylus that it scarcely fills a
paragraph. The two things we do know, with fair accuracy, are the dates
of his birth and death. One scholar records his birth as 525–24 BCE,
while another scholar follows that date with a question mark. As for the
death of the great man, there is no question: 456 BCE.

ELEUSIS AND THE MYSTERIES

Aeschylus was born in Eleusis, a city on the western coast of Attica, not
too many miles north of Athens. Eleusis had always been a significant
site, a strong prehistoric settlement that joined forces with Athens
sometime before the seventh century and became, by the end of the
sixth century, one of the major defenses of western Attica. Eleusis was
a center for many festivals of national and local importance, in
particular the yearly festival of the Eleusinian Mysteries. This highly
secret cult, dedicated to the two goddesses Demeter and Persephone,

This is the core of the book. The essay places the playwright in the context of his world and analyzes the influences and
inspirations within that world.

drew initiates from the entire Greek world, making the city one of Attica's most sacred spots and Athens' most famous deme, or political unit. Whether or not Aeschylus was an initiate of the Mysteries, he had a profound understanding of the cult.

THE FAMILY, THE CHILD, THE STATE

Aeschylus was born of an aristocratic family. As a boy he lived under the rule of Athenian tyrants, principally Pisistratus. These tyrants held down the aristocrats and were eventually overthrown by them. The aristocrats hoped to win back the rights of their nobility, but the new democracy led by Cleisthenes, himself an aristocrat, abolished both the tyrants and the long-entrenched aristocratic system. In its place rose a democratic state (the first in history) based on government by direct representation and local governance. It was in this new state that Aeschylus grew to manhood, a state that Werner Jaeger has described as "filled with all its high and earnest moral purpose."

FIGHTER FOR GREEK INDEPENDENCE

At the ages of thirty-five and forty-five, Aeschylus, fired by that "high and earnest moral purpose," fought in the two most important and defining battles Athens ever faced: Marathon in 490 and Salamis in 480, both the result of Persian invasions. "Few battles in history," writes Jaeger, "have been fought so entirely for the sake of an ideal as Marathon and Salamis." According to the historian Thucydides, Salamis was the battle "in which Athens established her future power and her aspirations to the hegemony of the whole Greek nation. . . . For Aeschylus, it was a revelation of the deep wisdom of the eternal justice which rules the world." At Marathon, the Athenian army and her allies numbered some 10,000 in contrast to double that number on the Persian side; and yet, only 192 Athenians died in battle as opposed to 6,400 Persians.

Athens and the entire Greek world had lived under the shadow of the threat of Persian domination since 514. It did not end until 480–79, at the battles of Salamis and Plataea, in which Aeschylus also fought, when the Persians were roundly defeated at sea in a battle between both nations' formidable navies. Aeschylus' description of this battle in *Persians* is the only surviving firsthand account of that historic event. This battle freed the Athenian state to become one of the cultural pinnacles in the history of Western civilization. Peter Green sums it up by saying that the Persian Wars "form a logical climax to the whole evolution of Greek society during the sixth century, an integral element in the intellectual revolution of Ionia and the political revolution at Athens." With this experience behind him, it is no wonder that Aeschylus concentrated on the theme of freedom versus autocracy in his plays.

THE FIRST VICTORIES IN TRAGEDY

Aeschylus produced his first tragedy in 499; he won his first prize for a tragedy in 484. Thereafter, he frequently won competitions in tragedy at the Great, or City, Dionysia, the annual Athenian religious festival that centered around the presentation of tragedy and eventually comedy, as well as other musical and choreographed events. Aeschylus won a total of thirteen first prizes. His first existing play, *Persians*, written in 472, was so successful that the Sicilian dynast Hieron invited him to restage it in Syracuse. Hieron also engaged him to write *Women of Aitna* in celebration of the founding of the city of Aitna. *Seven Against Thebes*, Aeschylus' second existing play, was first produced in Athens in 467 and was followed in 463 by the Danaid tetralogy. *Suppliants*, a part of the Danaid tetralogy, won first prize over Sophocles. *Oresteia*, the last play produced in Aeschylus' lifetime, was first performed at Athens in 458. In this tetralogy, he honored his beloved Athens and its bold experiment in democracy. Aeschylus then returned to Sicily, where he died in 456 at Gela, the place where he most likely wrote his final play, *Prometheus Bound*, produced post-humously by his son Euphorion.

The extent of Aeschylus' work is not certain, but it is likely to have been somewhere between seventy and ninety plays, a good number of which were tetralogies, three tragedies united by a single theme and followed by a satyr play that dealt comically with the same material. We know that he composed at least four tetralogies: the *Oresteia*, the Theban tetralogy, the Danaid tetralogy, and *Lycurgia*. Of these, only the *Oresteia* survives, though only as a trilogy (the satyr play having been lost), and one play each from the Theban and Danaid tetralogies. But from the names of the plays that have been lost, it is possible to reconstruct at least seven additional tetralogies.

The *Vita*, the ancient source that records the life of Aeschylus, notes that his epitaph does not mention his art but, as Sommerstein notes in *The Oxford Classical Dictionary*, refers "only to his prowess displayed at Marathon; this estimate of what was most important in Aeschylus' life — to have been a loyal and courageous citizen of a free Athens — can hardly be that of the Geloans and will reflect his own death-bed wishes . . . or those of his family."

EVOLUTION OF THEATER SPACE IN ATHENS

What was theater like during the time of Aeschylus? We know virtually nothing about it or about the origin of Athenian tragedy. We do know that the first performances of Athenian tragedy in the mid-sixth century took place in the *agora*, the Athenian marketplace, a place of general assembly, and that spectators sat on wooden bleachers. Then, around 500 BCE, the theatrical performance site was moved to the Sacred Precinct of Dionysus on the south side of the Acropolis. At first, spectators may have sat on the natural slope of the hill to watch the performance. Later, wooden bleachers were introduced for greater audience comfort. But even this is guesswork, logical as it sounds.

From here, we make a great leap to the middle of the fourth century, some 150 years into the future, to the theater at Epidaurus, perhaps the most aesthetically harmonious of all Greek theaters. There, a building called a *skene*, or stage, built in stone, served as a backdrop for the action. The stage had one to three doors fronted by a line of pillars, called the *proskenion*. Possibly, the stage had a second story and a *logion* — a roof for the appearance of gods and even mortals. In front of the stage was a raised terrace or low stage area where some if not most of the action took place. In front of that was the most crucial element of all, a perfectly round level space of pounded earth circled in stones called an *orchesis*, or orchestra — literally, "dancing space" — where the chorus would dance and sing and interact with the actors. Around the performance area was the *theatron*, or theater— a stone auditorium where the audience sat.

The stage at Epidaurus has no precedent in Athens until the 330s, when the *stoa* (covered walkways), stage, and theater were finally finished in stone. There is evidence, however, that the oldest stone stage in Athens dates from sometime between 421 and 415. And we know that for some years before that the stage was made of wood, torn down at the end of each festival and rebuilt (perhaps newly designed) the next year. Just when the first wooden stage was introduced is a mystery that may never find an answer; because of the fragility of these wooden structures and their demolition at the close of each festival, there are no archaeological remains.

About the only thing certain is that the plays of Aeschylus, which are the earliest existing plays of the Athenian Theater of Dionysus, require no stage building, which suggests that none existed. His earliest play, *Persians*, in 472, requires only a raised mound to serve as the grave or tomb of Darius. *Seven Against Thebes* needs only a representation of statues and altars of gods, and *Suppliants* requires much the same, except in place of statues of gods are symbolic representations of them. Some believe that *Suppliants* required a raised area to serve as a sanctuary for the chorus and for placing the symbols. This, however, is doubtfu,l as the chorus could not perform its choreographed dance on such a platform, which leaves us with a large playing area on a single level as the most logical possibility. *Oresteia*, in 458, is the first existing play of Aeschylus that requires a stage with at least one and perhaps more doors with a raised acting area in front.

But it is only in the late fifth and early fourth centuries that vase paintings of low, raised platforms for performing tragedy appear, suggesting their use at this time. This platform was raised about a meter (roughly forty inches) and mounted via a flight of steps in the center. The steps suggest that action was not confined to the platform but spilled out into the orchestra. This, of course, still tells us nothing about where the actors performed from the late sixth to well into the fifth century, nor is it conclusive evidence that such a raised level actually existed in Athens in the fifth century. Nothing short of archaeological evidence could do that, and of that there is none. From a purely practical standpoint, one must ask what would be the purpose of such a raised level, since the audience looked down on the action of the play from a steeply raked theater; even the first row of seats, the thrones for priests and dignitaries, was itself raised above the ground-level playing area of the orchestra.

ACTOR AND CHORUS ON EQUAL FOOTING

But there is another issue that goes beyond a question of sight lines, and that is the nature of Aeschylus' plays. They don't lend themselves to a separation between character and chorus, for the simple reason that it is precisely the relationship between them that is at the heart of the plays; they are inextricably bound together. Eteocles in *Seven Against Thebes* is who and what he is by virtue of his relationship with the people of his polis, his city; it is how they treat each other that determines what sort of hero Eteocles is, and that relationship has to be at close quarters. To see Eteocles on a raised platform speaking like any orator to the city, or criticizing the chorus from there, is unheard of if one has any real understanding of the nature of Aeschylus's play. The same is true of Clytemnestra and Agamemnon in *Oresteia*. For Agamemnon to enter at ground level and confront Clytemnestra on a platform a meter above him is to suggest that Clytemnestra needs elevation to maintain power, which weakens rather than strengthens her. If they meet at ground level, they appear as equals; Clytemnestra knows it even if Agamemnon doesn't. Tigers don't stalk their prey from a distance.

We also don't know the original shape of the early Athenian orchestra, where the chorus sang and danced elaborate choreographies. There are examples of smaller, outlying Attic theaters of the later fifth century whose orchestras were not circular. Both Thorikos and Trachones had tiny provincial theaters in which the audience was seated on wooden benches arranged in a rectangle close to the acting area, which may have been rectangular as well or, even more likely, trapezoidal, with only two sides parallel. It is possible that the early shape of the theater at Athens was the same, with the exception that it would have been on a much grander scale. Where does all this lead? Not much of anywhere except more speculation. Some scholars maintain, for example, that there is no evidence for a circular orchestra in Athens before the 330s. Others argue that the choreography performed by the chorus required a circular space, so there must have been one from the start. Who knows?

THEATER SIZE IN ATHENS

Whatever the layout of the early Athenian Theater of Dionysus, it is fair to assume that to accommodate the many male citizens from Athens and its outlying demes, not to mention important foreign visitors, the structure must have been sizable. And a large size meant spectators sat a great distance from the theatrical event. For example, the theater at Athens in the 330s rose to touch the fortified walls of the Acropolis some hundreds of feet away. The capacity of the theater has been judged to be somewhere between fifteen and twenty thousand.

THE MASK

Given the distance between spectators and actors, masks may have been used to provide the actors with greater visibility. Some have speculated that a mask served as a megaphone to project the voice to the farthest rows. The masks, which covered the entire head, at least gave a greater presence to the actor wearing one, whether or not they amplified the actor's voice. Made generally of linen, the fifth-century mask represented types rather than individuals.

There are other reasons why actors wore masks, however. Masks were a part of Greek culture and widely used, such as in cult ceremonies and in adolescent rites of passage. Puberty rites in Sparta made use of rather grotesque masks, and the cult of Demeter and Despoina at Lycosura used animal masks. Then, of course, there is the mask used in the cult of Dionysus, from which the mask in Greek tragedy most likely derives.

The rationale might also have been one of economy. Masks enabled an actor to be double and even triple cast, which meant only three actors with speaking parts were needed for a production. Masks were also helpful in disguising a male actor in a female role, as women were excluded from theatrical performances.

Even though the primary reason for having only three actors was very likely financial, to have the same actor play, for example, the roles of Clytemnestra, Electra, and Athena in *Oresteia* offered artistic and dramatic resonances that are far-reaching and intriguing. As for the number of nonspeaking actors onstage, there was no limit, and exciting stage effects with scores of "extras" would not have been unusual.

THE CHORUS

Of all the elements of Greek theater, the importance of the chorus cannot be overestimated. In Athens especially, there was a long tradition (even before tragedy) of choruses performing the dithyramb, an ancient Greek hymn sung and danced in honor of Dionysus, in competitions. Even in the days of tragedy, there were separate competitions devoted to the dithyramb in which each of the ten demes of Athens participated. In Aeschylus' day the tragic chorus numbered twelve, then Sophocles added three more, for a total of fifteen.

In his *Tragedy in Athens*, David Wiles proposes (with help from other scholars) that the choreographed movement of the chorus was particularly active and not highly formalized or in straight lines as previously thought. When, for example, the chorus of Young Theban Women in *Seven Against Thebes* makes its first entrance, it is anything but sedate; it is disordered in the extreme (choreographed disorder, to be sure). The women's terror of the encroaching war outside their city gates is such that it prompts the agitated reentry of Eteocles, who deals harshly with them for their civic disturbance. In Sophocles' *Oedipus at Colonus*, there is a similar entry by the chorus of Old Men, who dart wildly about the orchestra in search of the intruder into the Sacred Grove.

Wiles further proposes that the chorus acted out the subject of each choral ode in a choreographed dance. Chorus members not only wore the persona of Old Men of Colonus or Young Theban Women, they also acted out the subjects of others' narration. During long narrative speeches, such as the Persian Herald's speech in *Persians*, in which he describes the defeat of the Persian forces in the naval battle at Salamis, the chorus performed dances that visually complemented the narration.

Wiles' brilliant deduction indicates the broad and important role the choruses performed in Athenian tragedies. This expanded role explains why Athenians who attended the theater spoke of going to the choreography rather than to the play.

MUSIC AND TRAGEDY

We know very little about the music of Archaic and Classical Greece. Some music scores survive, but they are largely fragmentary and date from the Hellenistic period or later. Although the Greeks were knowledgeable about a great many musical instruments, especially from their eastern neighbors, they adopted only two types: a stringed instrument (lyre) and a wind instrument or pipe (aulos). The aulos was not a flute but a reed instrument (single and double). In fifth-century tragedy, the double-pipe aulos was the instrument of choice to accompany the musical sections of the dramatic action.

Music in the performance of fifth-century tragedy was of primary importance, and its similarity to modern opera has been noted. Every one of the existing tragedies has built into it a number of choral sections (usually five) that cover generally short passages of time and in which the singing and dancing chorus holds the center of attention in the orchestra. In addition, there are sections in which song is exchanged between characters, as well as an alternation between spoken dialogue and recitative or song, the latter often between a character or characters and the chorus. As Easterling rightly points out, these sections exist in the same time frame as the scenes of exclusively spoken dialogue — the rationale being "to intensify emotion or to give a scene a ritual dimension, as in a shared lament or song of celebration." How much music was used in performance is not known, but it is intriguing to speculate that its role was enormous and went far beyond those sections of the plays that call specifically for music.

THEATER FESTIVALS OF ATHENS

What we know about the production of tragedy in Greece is almost totally confined to Attica, though other areas were also active producers. In any event, from the close of the sixth and throughout the fifth century, tragedy was primarily performed as part of the Great, or City, Dionysia in Athens, though tragedy was also a part of the Rural Dionysia during the winter months, when bad weather made access to Athens difficult. But tragedy was not the sole reason for these festivals. They also included scheduled processions, sacrifices in the theater, libations, the parade of war orphans, and the performance of the dithyramb, comedy, and satyr play. The final day was devoted to reviewing the festival and awarding prizes.

Three tragedians competed with three plays each plus a satyr play, all chosen by the *archon*, a state official who also appointed the three *choregoi*, who undertook the expense of equipping and training the choruses. The actors and playwrights were paid by the state. One judge from each of the ten tribes, or demes, of Athens was chosen to determine the winners of the competition, and the winning playwright was crowned with a wreath of ivy in the theater. Until about the middle of the fifth century, the three tragedies of each day's performance comprised a trilogy; eventually each of the three plays had a different subject and were independent of one another, but always there was a satyr play.

And then there was Dionysus — god of theater.

DIONYSUS: GOD OF THEATER

What had the theater to do with Dionysus, and Dionysus with the theater? How did the two become one and mutually express one? Why is Dionysus an appropriate representative of the art of drama, and in particular of tragedy?

Aristotle conjectured that tragedy developed out of the dithyramb chorus. Since the subject of the dithyramb chorus was Dionysus, some scholars believe that tragedy simply kept Dionysus as the primary focus. Today, however, scholars are less certain about that succession, especially when one considers that tragedy deals with a broad range of subjects: Though Dionysus plays a significant part in tragedy, he has considerable competition.

Perhaps it is Dionysus' otherness — his ability to transform into animate and inanimate objects and his unpredictability — that makes him an appropriate representative for tragedy. Some say that his cult ritual, which existed long before tragedy, had aspects that formed the basis for drama: the use of masks for disguise; ecstatic possession, which included assuming alternate personalities; and mystic initiation. And then there is wine, discovered by Dionysus; the power of his ambivalent sexuality; and his association with dance and untamed nature. These are only a few of the possibilities that may have led to this god's association with drama.

The satyr play provides one clear link with Dionysus. From the late sixth and well into the fifth century, tragedy was associated with the satyr play, that light send-up of a classical mythological subject, and satyrs — those lusty half-goat, half-man creatures — were associated with Dionysus. As Easterling notes: The "satyr play . . . was the most obviously Dionysiac element, since the chorus of satyrs, far more than any other choral group, was explicitly and by definition part of the god's entourage, and satyrs of various types, as we have known from vase-paintings, had been associated with Dionysus well before the dramatic festivals were established."

DIONYSUS AND THE MASK

The theatrical mask suggests another link with Dionysus, as he is a god of escape, and the mask and theater itself provides an escape from daily life. But who would think of Greek tragedy as escapist fare, the means of leaving reality behind? And yet, Greek tragedy is filled with devices that separate it from daily life. Just as the Elizabethan playgoer didn't speak the language of Shakespeare's stage in the street, the diction and vocabulary of Attic tragedy was even more removed from the daily patter of the Athenian marketplace. In addition to the language, the music and the elaborate choreography of the chorus also provided theatrical distancing.

The mask permits an actor to take on not just one but as many roles as needed in the course of the tetralogy: the three tragic plays and the final comic satyr play. In the early days of tragedy there was one actor, then Aeschylus added a second, and Sophocles a third. No matter how many actors (one or three), each was required to play as many speaking roles as the plays called for, each time changing his mask to assume another character. Furthermore, each of the four choruses in a tetralogy would assume more than one identity, finally ending up as a band of cavorting and lascivious satyrs.

Pentheus, for example, in Euripides' play *Bacchae*, also plays his mother, Agave, who at the end enters carrying her son's severed head. No Athenian in that Theater of Dionysus could have failed to be aware of the game openly being played on him, and he must have relished it, knowing, by the timbre of a voice or by delivery, that Pentheus was now (in the terrible/wonderful deception that was theater) his mother carrying his own head. The illusion of reality was deliberately broken, which said to the audience that this is not life as you know it. And then there's always the down-and-dirty ribaldry of the satyr play to send the audience home laughing, just in case they fell into the trap of taking things a bit too seriously.

There is one further link between Dionysus and the mask. As we know from Greek pottery (in particular the large craters for storing wine), Dionysus was frequently "present" at cult rituals in the form of a large suspended or supported mask. The mask suggests that he served as an observer, watching the playing out of his many characteristics during the ritual. Similarly, at the beginning of every City Dionysia at Athens, a large statue of Dionysus was placed dead center in the theater to oversee the day's theatrical representations of the god in the form of transformation, disguise, ecstatic possession, and dance, and also in the satyr play and in general ribaldry and drunkenness.

And then there was sex.

DIONYSUS: GOD OF GENERATION AND FERTILITY

The sexual aspect of Dionysus and his cult is undeniable. His most formidable symbol is the giant phallus, a sign of generation and fertility. This ritual instrument was prominently displayed and carried through the streets in processions on various holidays. In a smaller form, as a piece of polished wood that resembled a dildo, it was placed in a cradle-like enclosure and treated like a baby at women's festivals.

As a subject for Attic tragedy, sex is prominent. It appears in one play after another as both a motif and a catalyst. It is so significant an element that Attic tragedy could scarcely do without it. One has only to think of Phaedra and Hippolytus, the Suppliants and their Egyptian suitors, Medea and Jason, Heracles and Deianira, Pentheus and Dionysus. In each of these relationships, sex is dark, disruptive, and tragic, and it leads inevitably to the resolution of all problems — death. Count no man happy until he is dead.

DIONYSUS, TRAGEDY, AND DEATH

Dionysus and death? The Dionysus who gives wine, who causes milk to flow from the earth and honey to spout from his ritual *thyrsus* (a staff of giant fennel covered with ivy and topped with a pine cone)? The god who carouses with his satyrs and maenads in the mountains? The answer can only be yes. Death, like sex, offers dissolution, escape, and liberation from the daily burdens of life. Both death and sex suggest rapture through destruction. Death is, after all, the only total escape, the only true liberation from pain, distress, dishonor, and fear, the only pure pleasure — and, at the same time, it is the paradoxical absence of that pleasure in nonbeing.

When we consider how often death is invoked in Athenian tragedy and how often it is the only answer to the dark shadow of sex, we realize that Dionysus is situated commandingly dead center in Athenian theater. He watches himself onstage in every act, from the playful to the tragic. He is not only observing from his place of honor but, like the gods in the various plays, manipulating the action and the fate of his characters — like Aphrodite and Artemis in *Hippolytus*, Athena in *Ajax*, or Dionysus himself in *Bacchae*. In the end, Dionysus is the god of the theater because he is everything: light/dark, hot/cold, sound/silence, pleasure/pain, life/death.

Dionysus lures his Athenian audience into his theater with a smile (he is, after all, known as the "smiling god," though at times demonically, eyes like spiraling pinwheels, tongue hanging from tightened lips). They come to escape reality; they want to be entertained with song and dance, poetry and masks. Theater is escape and illusion, with actors pretending to be multiple characters. But Dionysus knows what the theatergoers don't: They won't escape reality, rather reality will be heightened. Life is up there on his stage, a mirror of him, which is a mirror of all things — his all-encompassing fertility, including death. He is the god of theater, and specifically of tragedy, because in the end death is the only answer, and sex, life's greatest pleasure, becomes the catalyst that ultimately leads to death, the greatest pleasure of all.

PERSIANS

Except for the comedies of Aristophanes, Aeschylus' *Persians* is the only surviving play of fifth-century Athens to borrow its subject matter from contemporary history, as opposed to the usual sources: Homer's *Iliad* and *Odyssey* — those "bibles" of Greek life and religion — as well as from the even greater corpus of Greek mythology. *Persians* was first produced at the Great, or City Dionysia, in Athens in 472 and may have been meant to commemorate the Athenian victory over Persia at Salamis just eight years earlier.

The scene is laid at Susa, the Persian capital, and its action consists of four major incidents: the anticipation of news of the Persian expedition's fate; the arrival of a Herald with news of the Persians' defeat at Salamis; the raising of the Ghost of Darius, who criticizes his son's intemperate action; and the appearance of Great King Xerxes, the expedition's leader, now ragged, humbled, and disgraced.

TRAGEDY AND CONTEMPORARY HISTORY

About all we know from the written evidence is that *Persians* won first place for tragedy in 472 and that it is the first existing play of Aeschylus as well as the first surviving Athenian tragedy. One camp argues that the play is an unabashed self-congratulatory hymn of praise to the Athenian victory over the Persians. The other camp sees it as a faithful dramatization of a historical event, but criticizes Aeschylus for distorting the facts. Some question whether Aeschylus would have been permitted to use contemporary history as a subject matter, as opposed to myth and heroic legend. This issue is unsolvable for lack of evidence, but if the playwright was not allowed to use recent history, why was *Persians* not only accepted in its day but also very popular? A possible answer, one accepted by both sides of the issue, is that the extraordinary outcome of the Persian Wars eclipsed contemporary reality and rivaled divine myth and heroic legend: This historical event, because it was mythic in scope, had become a proper topic for a play.

HUBRIS-ATE

Aeschylus wove into his play the ancient law of *hubris-ate* — the moral lesson that pride leads to punishment (*ate*). As Herodotus says in his *Histories*: "God tolerates pride in none but himself." This concept is so ingrained in the Greek mind that it could be regarded as second nature. In retrospect, the Greeks would have seen the great Persian catastrophe at Salamis, Plataea, and Mycale as an example of this law. Aeschylus expresses this sentiment throughout *Persians* as a kind of refrain; a concept that all Greeks shared and one that more than likely opened up the Persian Wars as subject matter for the arts in the fifth century.

Hubris-ate is present from the beginning of *Persians*. The chorus of Old Men, those wise lords of Susa and advisers to the Great King, begins with a rousing opening hymn of praise for the expedition. But gradually, the chorus expresses doubts, until finally what began as extravagant praise ends with the thought of the price that must be paid for too much pride, for too great daring in the eyes of the gods. Out of the divinely ordained Persian destiny to wage war and tear down walls, to the glorious construction of the bridge of boats that straddles the Hellespont, arises the idea that the gods punish such extravagance. The gods' jealousy or envy is feared. Even the Herald speaks to Queen Atossa of the gods' jealousy of Xerxes' audacity, "Your son, at once, deceived by Greek treachery and the gods' jealousy . . . " he says; and a few lines later: "But little did he know the fate the gods had stored up."

BREAKING THE RULES?

When the Ghost of Darius rises from his grave, he speaks in no un-certain terms of the stupidity of his son's flagrant defiance of the gods' law, which keeps man in check, and of the consequence if man fails to obey. And later, when foretelling the Persian defeat at Plataea, Darius sees and describes the death and destruction that Xerxes' men will face, emphasizing again his son's rash decision to undertake the expedition.

Darius' expression of his disapproval could not be more harsh or clear; his words could have come from the mouth of a Greek — which, of course, since ultimately they came from Aeschylus, they did. Furthermore, Atossa, Xerxes' mother, within seconds of her first entrance, expresses an idea that was current in sixth- and fifth-century thought and related to the *hubris-ate* notion. As Ewans expresses it, it's "the idea that excessive wealth and prosperity may invite the jealousy of the gods, and those who go beyond their natural limits may be struck down."

This age-old Greek concept of *hubris-ate*, along with the larger-than-life, near-mythic actions and characters of the Persian Wars, is almost certainly what broke the (presumed) restriction on Greek tragedy of not performing contemporary historical events.

A MIGHTY ENDING

The last scene opens with the final chorus of Old Men, grandly dressed, again expressing Persia's greatness. Immediately after, Xerxes enters, his royal garments now ragged and torn. He arrives seated in a curtained carriage, but this time the curtain, designed to give shade and privacy, is tattered and torn, and the carriage is drawn by near-naked men, with a few soldiers straggling behind. The startling contrast between the past recalled just seconds before by the still richly dressed chorus and the ragged, humiliated, and despairing Xerxes and his equally ragged men is shattering.

From here to the end, everything is sung, with highly stylized choreography. The stylized nonverbal exclamations along with the music of the lyre and aulos create a scene of few words but powerful visual and aural components. It is packed with strange, alien Persian names: Pharandakes, Sousas, Pelagon, Agabatas, Pharnouchos, and Ariomardos.

The final scene is, in fact, a reversal on several levels of the play's initial scene. Both scenes begin with the chorus reciting the foreign (to Greek ears) names of men and places — praised in Scene One, mourned in the last scene. In the opening scene, the well-dressed chorus of Old Men enters, joined later by the pomp and pageantry of Atossa's spectacular entrance in a chariot, accompanied by a splendid host of grandly costumed servants, attendants, and bodyguards. No words could have conveyed a more powerful statement. Musically, too, there is contrast, from a proud, nationalistic song of praise to cries and lamentations accompanied by the shriek of the aulos. There is perhaps no scene so theatrically conceived in all Athenian tragedy.

As the play nears its conclusion, the lines spoken by Xerxes and the chorus grow shorter and shorter, until finally words all but fail and howls of agony and shame fill the scene. Aeschylus' audience, who had fought at Salamis and suffered the burning of Athens twice over, and for whom the ancient law of *hubris-ate* was so powerful, was no doubt profoundly moved by the tragic fate of the Persians to which each of them had contributed.

SEVEN AGAINST THEBES

Thebes is in a state of panic, anticipating an attack of an Argive army led by Polynices, brother of King Eteocles of Thebes, both of them the sons of Oedipus. Eteocles rebukes his people for their fear in the face of danger. He then names six of his generals to six of the seven gates of Thebes. Each appointment matches the Argive commander already assigned to that gate. When it is announced that Polynices will attack the seventh gate, Eteocles assigns himself to that location despite their father's curse that the brothers will kill one another. A Messenger recounts the battle won by the Thebans and describes the encounter of the two brothers in which each kills the other. The bodies of the two brothers, are brought in, and the play ends with a highly theatrical scene of lamentation.

FIRST MAN OF THE EUROPEAN STAGE

Seven Against Thebes begins with Eteocles, who serves as the dramatic focus of the action throughout the play. This differs markedly from both *Persians*, the play that precedes *Seven Against Thebes*, and *Suppliants*, the play that succeeds it. In those two plays, the chorus is the focal point.

Eteocles has been called by Kitto in his *Greek Tragedy*, "the first man of the European stage." Kitto singles out *Seven Against Thebes* as "our earliest tragedy of character." Eteocles is one of the most arresting figures of Athenian tragedy. He is the paradigm of the Heroic Man and one of the finest examples of the *arete* hero in existing Athenian tragedy.

ARETE: ALWAYS TO BE THE MOST NOBLE

Aeschylus treats Eteocles almost as a symbol, much as Shakespeare treats Henry V as a symbol of the ideal warrior king. It is not too much, perhaps, to say that Eteocles exemplifies what the Greek warrior of the fifth century strove to be — an embodiment of the concept of *arete*. This word goes back to the beginnings of Greece and is a major factor in the *Iliad* and the *Odyssey*.

The original meaning of *arete* was "warlike prowess." According to Werner Jaeger, in his *Paideia*, "its oldest meaning is a combination of proud and courtly morality with warlike valour." But by Homer's time, the word had broadened to mean exceptional ability and superiority. Or, to quote a line from Homer's *Iliad*, it is "to act always with valor, always to be the most noble." *Arete* combined noble action with the workings of a noble mind, which is another way of expressing the advice of Phoenix, the old teacher of Achilles, when he advises Achilles "to be both a speaker of words and a doer of deeds." Words and the ability to use words became a part of *arete* and were the sign of intellectual superiority.

The constant broadening of the meaning of *arete* is an indication of how Greek society kept expanding its ideals of human perfection, which were growing ever more exalted in terms of morals and honor. "Men," says Aristotle in *Nicomachean Ethics*, "seem to pursue honor in order to assure themselves of their own worth — their *arete*. They strive to be honored for it, by men who know them and who are judicious. It is therefore clear that they recognize *arete* as superior."

"Here, then," writes Jaeger, "we can grasp the vital significance of early aristocratic morality for the shaping of the Greek character. It is immediately clear that the Greek conception of man and his *arete* developed along an unbroken line throughout Greek history. Although it was transformed and enriched in succeeding centuries, it retained the shape that it had taken in the moral code of the nobility. The aristocratic character of the Greek ideal of culture was always based on this conception of arête," at the core of which is the highest form of self-love, which is to say not a self-aggrandizing love, but an altruistic one, the serving of others: an "ennobled self-love."

Aristotle will say much the same thing a century and a half later when he speaks of the *arete* hero, in his quest for the highest kind of self-love, as "taking possession of the beautiful. . . . For such a man would prefer short intense pleasures to long quiet ones; would choose to live nobly for a year rather than to pass many years of ordinary life; would rather do one great and noble deed than many small ones." And Jaeger concludes with, "The courage of a Homeric nobleman is superior to the berserk contempt of death in this — that he subordinates his physical self to the demands of a higher aim, the beautiful. And so, the man who gives up his life to win the beautiful, will find that his natural instinct for self-assertion finds its highest expression in self-sacrifice." This, then, is at the core of Aeschylus' Eteocles in *Seven Against Thebes*, for he chooses his own death in order to win his city's freedom rather than permitting himself to die because of his father's curse. In choosing his own death to save his people, he rises above the vulgar indignity of dying at the stroke of fate and, by doing so, takes possession of the beautiful.

This is what *Seven Against Thebes* is all about, and that alone makes it one of the noblest works in the history of not only Athenian tragedy, but Western theater. It is also an example of the frame of mind, or soul, in which the Athenian warrior — Aeschylus among them — approached the decisive and heroic battles of Marathon and Salamis. Like Eteocles, they were fighting out of self-love, which is to say *arete*; they were *arete* heroes defending their city and their city's and their own honor — the reward for which was to take possession of the beautiful.

SUPPLIANTS

The fifty Daughters of Danaus are in flight from their fifty Egyptian cousins, who are determined to marry them. The Daughters have just landed in Argos, their place of origin, only slightly ahead of the pursuing sons of Aegyptus. Pelasgus, the King of Argos, listens to their plea and finds himself in a dilemma. If he accepts the Daughters as new citizens of Argos, he risks war with the Egyptians; if he rejects them, he risks offending Zeus by being inhospitable. He therefore, along with Danaus, consults with the people of Argos and wins their support to accept the Daughters as citizens. A Herald from Aegyptus demands the Daughters' release, or the Egyptians will attach Argos. Pelasgus refuses and invites the new Argive citizens to their new home.

The Myth

The myth that Aeschylus chose to reinterpret in this tetralogy (of which *Suppliants* is the opening play) begins in the remote mythical past and is laid out in considerable detail in several of the odes sung by the chorus.

In this "superplot," as it has been called, the Argive princess Io, who is the keeper of the keys at Hera's temple in Argos, takes the fancy of Zeus, who amorously pursues her against her will. Hera, his wife, in a jealous rage turns Io into a cow. Zeus promptly assumes the form of a bull, causing Hera, in turn, to station as watch over Io the hundred-eyed giant Argos, who is then killed by Hermes and turned into a peacock. Hera, not to be outdone, retaliates by dispatching a gadfly to torment Io, who tries to escape by racing across continents, from Greece to Asia. She swims the width of the Bosporus (cow-ford) and finally reaches the Nile delta, where, in a meadow sacred to Zeus, she collapses in exhaustion. Zeus restores her to human form and, with a divine breath and a gentle touch (no sexual violence this time around), impregnates her with a son named Epaphus (meaning "touch or caress") who will become progenitor of a line of gods and heroes. Five generations later, two brothers, descended from Epaphus, fall into disagreement when one of them, Aegyptus, tries to force his brother Danaus to allow a marriage between his fifty sons and Danaus' fifty Daughters, at which Danaus, in fear and trembling, gathers his closely guarded brood and flees with them from Egypt to Argos, the land of their original mother, Io.

The Plea for Sanctuary

It is at this point that *Suppliants* begins, in the same marshy Argive meadow from which Io was once cruelly chased by Hera's gadfly. The scene is desolate except for a sacred mound, which serves as an altar sanctuary with symbols of Greek gods. It is to this sacred place that the chorus of Daughters will retire in their plea for sanctuary from the raging pursuit of their fifty Egyptian cousins. This plea for sanctuary is one of the two central subjects addressed by *Suppliants*, for it was a major issue in Aeschylus' time, as it had been from the earliest days of Greek civilization. It is also the core issue in several fifth-century Athenian tragedies, among them Sophocles' *Oedipus at Colonus*.

We are immediately introduced to the theme of sanctuary, or "guest-friend hospitality," as the Greeks called it. King Pelasgus enters with an escort of armed soldiers to investigate the Daughters' landing, and they appeal as suppliants in the name of their common Argive ancestry, a plea that places Pelagus in an agonizing bind. If he rejects their plea, he will offend Zeus as guardian of suppliants; and yet, if he accepts them, it means war with the pursuing Egyptian suitors.

The Daughters threaten to hang themselves from the symbols of the gods in the sacred precinct if Pelasgus won't give them sanctuary. Pelasgus, however, maintains that only the citizens' assembly can decide what to do, and off he goes with Danaus to gain the consent of the people of Argos. They, of course, agree unanimously, knowing full well that war with the Egyptians is likely. Guest-friend hospitality has won the day, though at considerable expense.

Flight from Sex and Marriage

The play opens with a choral ode sung by the Daughters. They inform us of their loathing for their pursuing suitors; they speak of "unholy marriage, loathsome, detestable, kinsmen, cousins, an unwanted marriage." The ode identifies the second subject that is central to *Suppliants*, and to which the Athenian audience of the time would have responded with considerable interest: sex, which is the motivating factor in the play as a whole. The Daughters' loathing of their male cousins and their terror at the prospect of marriage recurs so often in the play that it assumes the aspect of phobia — particularly if one realizes that marriage within a family group was in no way unusual for the Classical Greeks.

We also learn that it was not the young women themselves who instigated the flight from marriage but their old father, Danaus, who "advised this rebellion as the best of the evils that promise sorrow." They agreed, calling themselves "willing fugitives." Throughout the play, they will constantly refer to sex in derogatory terms: "Death before they foul this marshy land! . . . Kill them before they make our beds unholy, before they mount our beds of innocence . . ." They appeal to Justice and hate the "pride" (hubris) of their pursuers, pleading that "force" not make their marriage bed. They then invoke Artemis as defender of chastity to come to their aid. And if the sky gods fail to heed their pleas to be saved from marriage and sex with their cousins, they declare that they will invoke the "Zeus of the world below, Hades" and hang themselves from the symbols of the gods in the sacred precinct. Zeus, it must be noted, is mentioned unusually often in this play, and for a good reason: In effect, he is their father. It was his breath and gentle caress that made him the father of Epaphus, Io's son, and the progenitor of their line; they are "children" of Zeus.

FATHER DOESN'T KNOW BEST

Their opening lyric concluded, their father, Danaus, speaks, and we learn very quickly that he is an old man of much advice. We already know that he advised the flight of his fifty Daughters, and early in his first speech, we also discover that he wants them to "write his words" in their hearts or minds and to heed them. And he ends his speech with advice on how to speak and behave when the Argives come to inquire regarding their presence on Argive shores.

Sounding a bit like a tedious Polonius, Danaus gives us the impression of advising a bit too much where his young Daughters are concerned, and frequently on sexual matters. When he speaks of modesty and tells them to keep their eyes downcast at all times, he is telling them not to flirt or look with too much interest on the Argive men who will come to question them. Immediately, they respond like worshipful, dutiful Daughters: "Your words are wise, father, and spoken to Daughters who respect wisdom. We won't forget." Immediately following these words, they invoke Zeus with: "And may Father Zeus, our first father, look down upon us!" There are times, as here, when the margin between Danaus and Zeus is so close as to be indistinguishable, a father-worship that suggests the Daughters' fear of sex and marriage may have as much to do with Danaus' overprotection as with their impulsive cousins.

Danaus' "advice" and the Daughters' constant need for it continues to the end of the play. They have won the Argive people's support and are invited into the city to live wherever they choose, yet they need their old father's advice, and they ask Pelasgus "one more favor. Send our brave-hearted father to advise us. He's wise and we listen to his counsel. He'll know best where we should live." He arrives, and in the course of his final lengthy speech reveals some facts concerning his fatherly protectiveness. Early on he begins as we have heard him before: "Listen to me again now; and to the other wisdom I have given you, write these words in your memory."

They are foreigners, he tells them, and must manage themselves well or risk criticism from the people of Argos. But most important of all to him is the sexual demeanor of his young Daughters. The imagery of his speech is wonderfully expressive, and critics have rightly been thrilled by its delicate, nuanced beauty. And yet there is something devious about his words of advice.

Nature imagery in his speech takes on a not unconventional reference to female sexuality: the plunder of those fruits by animals, birds, and beasts, "as well as men." What else can one expect of predators? he concludes. Men, conquered by the sight of beauty, enter Aphrodite's garden of delights to seduce. Again, he might ask, what else can one expect? Men will be men. So far so good. He has presented a ravishingly beautiful description of the inevitability of sex and love. But then comes the thorn in the finger. So far Danaus has spoken objectively, but now his advice to his virginal Daughters becomes subjective and limiting. He tells them that despite sex's inevitability, it serves them best to guard their treasure. And what else should we expect of the chorus of Daughters, represented by the chorus leader, than: "I pray the great gods to rain down good fortune upon us! As for my summer fruit, father, unless the gods have laid new plans, my path is set."

What else can "my path is set" mean but that sex will not be a part of their lives? Is it too much to say that old Danaus has brainwashed his Daughters into an antisexual mode? The advice he gives them so liberally in the play can't be new; they've heard it for years. And one can hardly ignore that at the end of the second play of the tetralogy, or between the second and the third (an assumption, since neither still exists), the Egyptian cousins are murdered by their new wives in the bridal chamber on their wedding night. It is not difficult to conclude that the influence of Danaus on his Daughters is disastrous.

The Athenian citizen sitting in the Theater of Dionysus watching *Suppliants* would have had little trouble coming to the same conclusion. It was the Classical Greeks' heritage to view sex as a natural function to be healthily engaged in. In Athens, at least, there was an unwritten law that a male was expected to marry by age forty at the latest. Aeschylus leaves no doubt where he, as a Classical Athenian, stands on the issue. In the final scene, the chorus of Argive Women enters with Pelasgus and his soldiers, singing the praises of love, marriage, and sex, of "love's whispers and cries and the gentle touching of flesh." The Daughters respond by pleading with Zeus to "spare us from a hateful marriage to men who are loathsome enemies. . . . I pray for innocence, in Justice's name." The Argive Women counsel them "To pray a more moderate prayer."

ORESTEIA

Oresteia was written at the height not only of the life of Aeschylus, but at the height of the glory of Athens, still basking in the glow of its victory over Persia in 480–79, and in the train of its accomplishments in art, sculpture, architecture, philosophy, poetry, tragedy, and, not least, democracy. More, Aeschylus wrote *Oresteia*, his greatest work, when he was in his late sixties, only two years before his death in 456. It is not difficult to see this play as his final tribute to the greatness of Athens and its people. It is a work of such scope and magnitude that it has never, from the date of its conception in 458 to today, been superseded in majesty, power, and moral rectitude. So splendid is it in its moral integrity that it is in keeping with those other central triumphs of Athenian greatness, Marathon and Salamis. And its moral foundation is nothing less than what Aeschylus saw as the foundation of Athens and her people.

 Agamemnon, the first play of the *Oresteia* trilogy, opens in the dead of night, and the trilogy ends in a glow of light with a torchlight procession lighting the former Furies, now the Eumenides, or the Kindly Ones, to their new home as guardians of Athens and her people. That succession from dark to light is more than a theatrical ploy; it is a metaphor for the evolution of the Greek world from superstition to enlightenment, from chaos, where blood justice and vengeance rule, to order through law and moral justice. The transformation of the Furies into the Kindly Ones is an embodiment of that progress. They represent a society that founded the Areopagus, the Athenian court, and the world's first trial by jury. The topic of oppression and tyranny, which preoccupied Aeschylus, is at the foundation of *Oresteia*, where we see humankind progress from blind instinct to reason.

Agamemnon and the Purple

Agamemnon opens on the palace roof, where a Watchman waits for a signal announcing the fall of Troy. Ten years have elapsed since the Greeks sailed to war. He sees the signal and, jubilant, tells the good news to the household. A chorus of Old Men of Argos enters to report that all the altars in the city are ablaze with sacrificial offerings. They recount the story of Iphigenia, daughter of Agamemnon, who sacrificed her at Aulis so that his fleet could sail to Troy. They then call on Queen Clytemnestra, wife of Agamemnon and regent in her husband's absence, to explain the burning altars. She tells them of the fall of Troy. At first skeptical, they are won over. They sing of Helen and Paris and of the grief and civil unrest that this empty war has brought to Greece.

A Herald arrives announcing the imminent return of Agamemnon, victorious, from Troy. The Old Men hint darkly that all is not well in Argos, but Clytemnestra sends the Herald back with a message of welcome for Agamemnon. Before going, however, the Herald reveals that most of the Greek fleet has been lost in a terrible storm on the voyage home. The chorus sings of the evils of Helen.

Agamemnon arrives in a chariot, with Cassandra, a Trojan priestess of Apollo and his captive. The chorus welcomes him, again hinting that those who seem faithful may have something to hide. Agamemnon salutes the city's gods, describes his victory at Troy, and determines to enter the palace. Instantly, Clytemnestra stalls him.

Having declared her faithfulness to him, and her relief at seeing him safely home, she informs him that she has sent their son, Orestes, to an ally for safekeeping against possible revolt in Mycenae. She then orders slaves to lay out a rich purple tapestry carpet between Agamemnon's chariot and the palace doors so that Agamemnon can enter in kingly dignity. Agamemnon appears offended. The tapestries are expensive. To damage them by stepping on them would be wasteful and arrogant; it would incur the disapproval of the city and the wrath of the gods. Clytemnestra persuades him that, as conqueror of Troy, he deserves no less. She asks him to walk on the tapestries as a concession to her. As he does so, she expresses her pleasure at his homecoming. The chorus is full of foreboding, however. They sense that something is terribly wrong.

Clytemnestra then instructs Cassandra to enter the palace too. Cassandra is agitated, but says nothing. Clytemnestra enters the palace, leaving Cassandra with the chorus. Cassandra suddenly bursts into sounds of lament, directed at Apollo, the god who does not accept laments. The chorus is distressed by this ill omen. They know that Cassandra is a princess of the royal house of Troy. Gradually, as Cassandra becomes more comprehensible, she reveals that, because she accepted and then rejected Apollo's sexual advances, he first gave her the gift of prophecy and then cursed her so that, while she would accurately foretell the future, no one would believe her. She was able to foresee the doom of Troy, but not stop it. She knows the bloody history of the House of Atreus and prophesies that Clytemnestra is even now preparing to kill Agamemnon inside the house, and Cassandra with him. She rips off the prophetic garments of Apollo and tramples them underfoot. Knowing that she cannot escape death, she approaches the palace, but recoils at the horrors within. Steeling herself once again for death, she finally enters.

The chorus barely has time to draw breath before Agamemnon is heard to cry out. The chorus panics. It realizes what is happening, but it cannot agree on whether to storm the palace or wait for further information. Clytemnestra appears, spattered with blood, and the bodies of Agamemnon and Cassandra are displayed. He has been hacked down with an axe like a sacrificial animal and wrapped in a netlike material. Clytemnestra now openly declares her hatred for him and her joy at having paid him back for the death of their daughter, Iphigenia. There is a bitter exchange with the chorus, during which she tries to justify herself by invoking the curse on the House of Atreus. The chorus is not convinced.

Finally, Aegisthus arrives with a cohort of guards. To justify his part in the plot to kill Agamemnon, he recounts the gruesome story of the child-banquet in which all his brothers perished. The chorus accuses him of cowardice for having left the killing to a woman. He threatens them with death unless they show him respect. A near massacre is averted by Clytemnestra, who persuades Aegisthus to ignore the Old Men and enter the palace with her to begin their reign.

Libation Bearers: **The Homecoming**

The second play, *Libation Bearers*, takes place some ten years later, when Orestes, son of Clytemnestra and Agamemnon, now a young man, returns from exile to avenge his father's murder. He is with his companion-mentor-lover, Pylades, whose father has raised Orestes from childhood. Orestes places a lock of his hair on his father's grave as a funeral tribute. As Electra, Orestes' sister, and a chorus of Women Captives from Troy approach, Orestes and Pylades hide. Clytemnestra has had an ominous dream and has sent Electra and the chorus to the grave of the dead king to propitiate him with prayers and libations. Instead, the chorus of women convinces Electra to pray for the return of Orestes as avenger. Pouring the libations on the grave mound, she notices the lock of hair and footprints, which she believes are those of her brother.

At this point, Orestes reveals himself to her and proves his identity by showing her a piece of tapestry that she had woven for him when he was a child. He tells her of Apollo's command to avenge his father and of how he will be severely punished if he fails to do so. Together, brother, sister, and chorus pray at length to summon the vengeful spirit of Agamemnon, until they are convinced that the dead king has heard them and will aid them from beyond the grave. Orestes then lays out his murder plan. Pylades, Orestes, and Electra leave, and the chorus sings of the wickedness of women in the past and of the advent of Justice.

Following the ode, Orestes and Pylades return disguised as travelers from Phocis. After a brief encounter with the Gatekeeper, Clytemnestra enters. They tell her that Orestes has died in exile. Believing their story, she welcomes them into the palace. Cilissa, the nurse who tended Orestes as a baby, enters in tears at the news of his death. She has been sent to fetch Aegisthus and his bodyguard. The chorus, however, has no trouble persuading her to have Aegisthus come alone. Aegisthus arrives following a choral ode and proceeds into the palace. Not long after, an offstage cry announces his death. Clytemnestra enters to face Orestes. With the encouragement of Pylades (who speaks his only three lines in the entire play at this point), Orestes forces Clytemnestra, step by step, back into the palace.

After an ode of joy sung by the chorus, the doors open, and Orestes is seen standing over the bodies of Clytemnestra and Aegisthus. Orestes orders slaves to throw down the netlike tapestry robe used in the murder of his father so that all can see it. Unlike Clytemnestra in *Agamemnon*, who stood over the bodies of her husband and Cassandra, elated and proud of her conquest, Orestes expresses only anger, then sadness, and finally frenzy as in his mind's eye he sees his mother's Furies closing in on him. Tortured by the vision, he sets out for Delphi to seek Apollo's protection. The chorus wonders when the suffering will end.

The Great Transformation

The final play of the trilogy, *Eumenides* (the Kindly Ones), opens in front of the temple of Apollo at Delphi. The Prophetess Pythia prays before beginning the day's activities and enters the temple, only to crawl out a moment later in a state of terror. In the god's sanctuary, she says, is a man dripping blood, and surrounding him a swarm of sleeping female Furies too horrible to be endured. She summons Apollo before leaving. Apollo and Orestes enter. The god sends Orestes on a journey that will last years and end with his arrival at Athens.

While the furies sleep, the vengeful spirit of Clytemnestra appears in their dreams, instructing them to pursue Orestes. The Furies awake in Apollo's temple, only to be confronted by Apollo, who threatens them with his bow and arrows and expels them from his sanctuary. They round on him for encouraging Orestes to commit matricide and for ignoring their ancient rights. After a brief exchange, the Furies leave in pursuit of Orestes.

The scene changes to the Athenian Acropolis and the monumental statue of Athena, where Orestes, after his lengthy wanderings, seeks sanctuary. Almost immediately, the Furies enter and surround him. Ignoring his claims that he has been purified of all blood-pollution, they begin to sing a song of power that will bind and destroy him. At this point, Athena enters. She determines that only a trial can settle the issue. She leaves to select a jury of the best Athenian male citizens.

Following a song by the Furies, we understand that the scene has now moved to the Areopagus, the Hill of Ares, next to the Acropolis, where the trial begins. The Furies serve as prosecution, Apollo as defense. The issue is matricide: Can a son kill his mother to avenge his father? Before the vote is taken, Athena establishes the institution of trial by jury and the principles of justice for all time. The jurors vote, but threatened on one side by the Furies, who vow to curse Athens should they lose the vote, and on the other by the power of Zeus, represented by Apollo, the vote is even. Athena exercises her right to cast the tie-breaking vote, and Orestes is acquitted.

Orestes in gratitude pledges his and his city's eternal friendship with Athena. The Furies protest the injustice of the decision, enraged that their age-old rights have been usurped by the new gods of Olympus. Appealing to Night, their mother, they threaten to blight the land of Athens. However, over a lengthy scene, Athena calmly persuades them to relinquish their claims and accept an honored place in the Athenian state, where they will forever be worshipped as fertility goddesses and protectors of justice and live in the rock beneath the Areopagus, the site of the court. A triumphant musical dialogue follows between the Furies and Athena. Now transformed from Erinyes (Furies) to Eumenides (Kindly Ones), they are dressed in purple robes by a chorus of Athenian women and girls. The trilogy ends as they leave in a blaze of flaming torches, with a song blessing their new home. Justice has been served, fertility is the land's blessing, and civic peace is established.

Sexy Goat-Men End the Day

There then followed a satyr play: a burlesque, mock-tragic play involving a combination of "serious" mythological characters and satyrs (bibulous, sexually avaricious goat-men). Each tragedian wrote a satyr play to follow his trilogy of tragedies as a light-hearted end to a long day's theatergoing. Although we have many tragedies, only one satyr play — the *Cyclops* by Euripides — survives. We know the satyr play that Aeschylus wrote to follow the *Oresteia* was called *Proteus*, and it may have dramatized the story of how Menelaus and three of his companions disguised themselves as seals to trap the shape-changing, prophetic sea-divinity, Proteus.

PROMETHEUS BOUND

Fire, it is safe to say, is essential to civilization. It protects us from the cold. It cooks the food we eat. And it makes possible the transformation of the natural world that surrounds us to serve our needs. There is no mythology that doesn't in some way memorialize its advent. In some cases, a bird, an animal, or even a man steals this divine spark from the gods. From the Far East to the North American Far West, from the Arctic to the Antarctic, it is everywhere embedded in the human collective unconscious. In the *Rig-Veda*, the oldest and most sacred of the Hindu Vedas, the god Matarisvan, by rubbing, gives birth to the fire-spirit Agni and then introduces him to earth. In Greece it is the pre-Olympian Titan Prometheus who serves the earth's population in that function.

THE CRUELTY OF ZEUS

Prometheus Bound is set somewhere near the beginning of time on a desolate mountain crag in Scythia in the Caucasus. Cratus (Power) and Bia (Violence), functionaries of a tyrannical Zeus, enter dragging the rebel Titan god Prometheus. With them is Hepheastus, the god of fire and metal smithing, who, at the brutal insistence of Cratus, chains Prometheus to the mountain crag. Isolated, he is visited by a chorus of the Daughters of Oceanus. He first hints that he knows of a conspiracy that threatens Zeus, but he says he will not reveal it until he is freed and granted redress for his wrongful punishment. He then recounts his crimes against Zeus: He thwarted Zeus' plan to destroy the human race. He also gave humanity hope in the face of death and fire. This exposition is interrupted by a visit from a fellow Titan, Oceanus, father of the chorus, who offers to serve as intermediary between Prometheus and Zeus, an offer that Prometheus rejects. Then Io enters, a human victim of Zeus' cruel lust; she is half girl, half cow, forced to wander the earth, driven to a frenzy by a gadfly — a vivid testimony of Zeus' cruelty to the despised race of mortals. Io exits, and Prometheus tells the chorus that he knows of a potential marriage that would lead to Zeus' downfall. Soon after he says this, Hermes, Zeus' messenger, appears and tells Prometheus that unless he reveals who threatens to overthrow Zeus, he will be plunged into the bowels of earth, only to be brought back to light so that Zeus' eagle can eat his liver. Prometheus refuses, and at the play's conclusion, the earth opens in a cataclysmic storm of earth and sky, and Prometheus is engulfed.

The Unseen Presence

Of the two main characters of this play, one of them, Zeus, doesn't appear. (It is noteworthy that Zeus appears in no existing Greek tragedy and possibly never in any play.) Nonetheless, a portrait of Zeus is so vividly drawn that he is as present as the onstage Prometheus, chained to his rock. Zeus is a tyrant, pure and simple, and Aeschylus wastes no opportunity in defining him as that at every turn. We may not see Zeus, but we see his henchmen, Cratus, Bia, Hepheastus, and Hermes, at work. We also see the effects of his tyranny — Prometheus chained to the crag and Io suffering a cruel persecution, as well as the more general suffering of humanity. What's more, even the gods of Olympus are subject to Zeus' tyranny. In his opening command to Hepheastus, Cratus says that Prometheus must learn to accept Zeus' "sovereignty," a euphemism for tyranny. Hepheastus, who pities Prometheus and resists chaining him to the crag, notes that even the gods aren't free, and Cratus agrees. They all are slaves; they all know pain — all except Zeus, the god at the top. "Only Zeus is free," Hepheastus concludes.

Zeus as Tyrant

Tyrants were not unknown to Archaic and Classical Greece; however, the concept of tyrant changed over time. As M. I. Finley defines it:

"Originally a neutral word, 'tyrant' signified that a man seized and held power without legitimate constitutional authority (unlike a king); it implied no judgment about his quality as a person or ruler." A tyrant could be a good man, as he was in the early days of Greek civilization. Oedipus was in that sense both a tyrant and a good man.

It is intriguing that Aeschylus' description of Zeus as a bad and oppressive tyrant anticipates the first clear and modern definition of the tyrant in Greece by approximately a century. It was not until the middle of the fourth century that Aristotle, by studying past tyrannies and observing current ones, laid out in vivid terms the characteristics of the bad tyrant in his book *Politics*.

But it is a short passage in Aristotle's *Rhetoric* that provides a succinct description of Zeus as he appears in Aeschylus' play. "This tyranny," writes Aristotle, "is just that arbitrary power of an individual which is responsible to no one, and governs all alike, whether equals or better, with a view to its own advantage, not to that of its subjects, and therefore against their will. No freeman willingly endures such a government." We find not only Aeschylus' Zeus in that statement but Prometheus as well — the freeman who cannot willingly endure such a government.

Other powerful men, or men of noteworthy achievements and determination, are also the enemies of the tyrant. These men are the most likely to conspire against him. "Some," says Aristotle, "because they want to be rulers themselves; others because they do not want to be slaves." The wise tyrant, the one who wants to maintain his tyranny, takes seriously the advice of Periander: Lop off the heads, from time to time, of outstanding citizens. Concerning Prometheus, Zeus would likely gladly follow Periander's advice, except that Prometheus, being a god, isn't susceptible to death — a point Prometheus himself makes to the Daughters of Oceanus when indicating the length of his suffering.

The profound distrust of the tyrant even by his peers leads him, as Aristotle notes, "to get regular information about every man's sayings and doings. This entails a secret police [sent] to all social gatherings and public meetings. Men are not so likely to speak their minds if they go in fear of a secret police; and if they do speak out they are less likely to go undetected." What else can we call Hermes near the play's conclusion but an eavesdropper, a member of Zeus' secret police, a spy? His arrival is swift, suspiciously swift, after the news from Prometheus that Zeus will be overthrown because of an event still to come, which only Prometheus knows of.

Unwitting Complicity

And then there is Oceanus — friend, Titan relative, once involved with Prometheus in his reforms. He enters the scene on his winged monster like a figure in a medieval morality play. He isn't quite like a villain or devil tempting the virtuous Christian to betray his faith, but he bears some similarity.

Oceanus certainly doesn't see himself as a tempter trying to subvert his friend's integrity. His motivations are honorable, at least in his own eyes, and his intentions are better than Satan's. He sees submission as the most politic way of saving his own (and his Titan friend's) skin: Do as Oceanus advises and you will survive. He believes what he says to Prometheus; he wants simply, in his simple way, to help his friend and fellow Titan see reason and save himself.

The problem with Oceanus is that he is lazy minded as well as lazy spirited. His advice, if followed, would lead Prometheus to complicity with the enemy, which is unacceptable to Prometheus. Oceanus, in his nonintrusive, apolitical, unquestioning path, is, for Prometheus, a sycophant, a courtier.

How else does one understand Prometheus' response to Oceanus' "survival" tactics other than as ironic, particularly when it is couched in deceptively non-inflammatory language? To Oceanus' "The only thing, I think, you've never learned is that foolish words never escape punishment," Prometheus responds with deceptive friendliness: "How lucky you are! You dared with me, you shared with me. Everything. And yet you're free of blame and punishment. I envy you. Stay out of it. You're only heading for trouble. He won't change. His mind is set. Persuasion will get you nowhere."

Oceanus, of course, isn't quick-witted enough to perceive irony when it stares him in the face, and he replies with: "You're better at advising others than yourself." Prometheus then thanks Oceanus for his offer to mediate for him with Zeus. Oceanus doesn't realize that Prometheus as hero — passionate in his need to defend honor, freedom, and personal as well as societal integrity — cannot survive by simply "surviving."

On Knowing Oneself

"Know yourself," said Oceanus to Prometheus early on: a splendid adage of the Greek world, widely admired, inscribed on Apollo's temple at Delphi. The irony here, of course, is that Prometheus *does* know himself, knows why he was born and knows why he has done what he has done and will continue to do: oppose tyranny. It is nothing less than that knowledge that makes Prometheus what he is. That knowledge makes Oceanus evil not only in the eyes of Prometheus but in those of Aeschylus and of the fifth-century Athenian males seated in the Theater of Dionysus on that spring day.

Showing the Tragedy

The entrance of Io, unexpected, out of nowhere, considered by many a scene largely unrelated to the play, is perhaps the most brilliant of Aeschylus' innovations. He is again, as in *Seven Against Thebes* and *Suppliants,* not only telling but showing his audience the subject of his tragedy. Io exemplifies tyrannical injustice, from which both she and Prometheus suffer.

Here is Io, the helpless and unwilling victim of Zeus' predatory lust, a young woman whose very body is gruesomely deformed and who is driven mad by the gadfly's sting and condemned to a terror-stricken flight across continents. It is the play's longest scene, and like the "shield" scene in *Seven Against Thebes*, the one that expresses most concretely the play's central concern — the horror and injustice of tyranny. The audience sees the pain of Io, and that, along with the sight of the "crucified" Prometheus, hammers home the playwright's theme.

Endurance Is All

Prometheus knows firsthand how Zeus' regime operates, just as he knows the nature of Hermes' mission. "Kowtowing ass-wipe of the latest tyrant," he calls him, and later, "Make no mistake: nothing could make me trade my misery for your servility." Angered, Hermes tries every means of breaking Prometheus' spirit, but fails, only to become even more enraged. He describes Prometheus as "a young colt, new-harnessed, straining at the bit, struggling, bucking, fighting the reins" and reminds him of the pain he will endure unless he relents. Finally, Hermes agrees to the inevitable, accepts that Prometheus will not give up, and dismisses him as mad, his reason lost. He warns the chorus to leave or risk sharing Prometheus's fate. But the chorus angrily denounces Hermes, saying they will not be persuaded to baseness and dishonor. And with that, Hermes departs — and Prometheus endures.

DRAMATIC MOMENTS

from the Major Plays

Agamemnon (**458** BCE)   **42**

Agamemnon (**458** BCE)   **49**

Libation Bearers (**458** BCE)   **53**

Eumenides (**458** BCE)   **67**

Prometheus Bound (**456** BCE)   **72**

These short excerpts are from the playwright's major plays. They give a taste of the work of the playwright. Each has a short introduction in brackets that helps the reader understand the context of the excerpt. The excerpts, which are in chronological order, illustrate the main themes mentioned in the In an Hour essay.

from **AGAMEMNON** (458 BCE)

[The Trojan War is over. A victorious Agamemnon is returning home. Unknown to him, Clytemnestra, his wife, is both unfaithful and bitter at his sacrifice of their daughter Iphigenia to gain favorable passage for his ships on the way to Troy. Clytemnestra is plotting Agamemnon's murder.]

CHARACTERS

>First Old Man
>Clytemnestra (Klytaimnêstra)

(Outside the palace at Mykenê.)

FIRST OLD MAN:
Majesty —

>queen —

>Klytaimnêstra —

we come here in respect of your
>power and authority.
For when the king is away
>and the throne empty of the male,
>>it is only right that the
>>honor that we owe to him
>should fall to his woman —
>>his wife —
>>our queen.

Majesty.

May I ask the reason for these flaming altars
>here and throughout the city?

Is there news?

Good or bad?

Or is it rumor?

Another empty hope that brings this sacrifice?

I long to know, lady.

Loyal as I am.

But if not —

we respect your silence

KLYTAIMNÊSTRA:

As the proverb has it:

"May Dawn,

coming from her mother Night,

bring glad tidings."

The news I bring beggars all hope.

Troy has fallen.

Priam's citadel is taken.

The Greeks are in Troy.

FIRST OLD MAN:

Troy taken? I can scarcely believe it.

KLYTAIMNÊSTRA:

Yes, Troy taken. I say what I mean.

FIRST OLD MAN:

The joy of this news — my eyes — my tears —

KLYTAIMNÊSTRA:

The tears of a loyal servant, yes.

FIRST OLD MAN:

But Troy fallen? Have you proof?

KLYTAIMNÊSTRA:

I have; unless some god has deceived me.

FIRST OLD MAN:

Perhaps some dream you dreamed deceived you.

KLYTAIMNÊSTRA:

I believe in dreams no more than you.

FIRST OLD MAN:

Rumor, then, some unfounded report.

KLYTAIMNÊSTRA:

I'm not a young girl! I won't be insulted!

FIRST OLD MAN:

Yes, well. And Troy was taken when?

KLYTAIMNÊSTRA:

Last night, I told you!
Last night that gave birth to this
burst of light.

FIRST OLD MAN:

Was the news winged to arrive so fast?

KLYTAIMNÊSTRA:

Winged?

No, better yet, and faster.
Fire.
A courier of fire,
from peak to peak,
from Troy to Argos,
beacon signals from fire-god Hêphaistos.
In the flash of an eye,
it sped from Ida to Hermês Crag on Lêmnos,
then leapt to Athos, where the Rock of Zeus
took flame in the night,
and rising high above the sea's back,
a speeding torch,
a second sun,
it brought its dazzling news to the heights of Makistos.
The watchers, awake,

waste no time in feeding the flame
and speeding it across the waters of Euripos
to the sentinels waiting on Messapion.
There they kindle an answering flame
with heather and dry brush,
till it blazes to the shame of its predecessor,
then leaps like a brilliant moon,
across the Plains of Asopos
to light on the peaks of Kithairon,
igniting fire after fire
that flashes the news on its course.
And the distant flame is not rejected by the watch,
but urged onward beyond the Swamp of the Gorgon
to the Mountain of Roving Goats,
where the watch does itself proud.
Sparing nothing,
they set blazing a mountain of kindling
that shakes its great head of flaming hair
and soars out across the headland
that looks down upon the Gulf of Saron,
then down and down to Spider Peak,
the watchpost nearest our city —
and,

in one final leap,
plunges to the roof of this palace
of the sons of Atreus.

This is my proof!
This my certainty!
Fire upon fire upon fire,
a relay race of flame,
sent me by my king from the blaze at Troy,
my husband,

Agamemnon.

FIRST OLD MAN:

>The gods will have their thanks in time, lady,
>
>>but first, because what you say is such a marvel,
>>
>>>I'd be grateful to hear your fable told again.

KLYTAIMNÊSTRA:

>What is it you don't grasp?
>
>>>>Troy is taken.
>>
>>It's as simple as that.
>>
>>Taken today.
>>
>>By the Greeks.
>
>And Troy is today a city of cries,
>
>>cries that refuse to blend,
>>
>>>like vinegar and oil,
>>
>>eternal contestants:
>>
>>>>Greek and Trojan,
>>
>>>victor and vanquished,
>>
>>cries as different as their fortunes differ.
>
>Trojans mourn husbands and brothers,
>
>>parents,
>>
>>>children;
>>
>>>>a keening lament
>>
>>from throats no longer free,
>>
>>mourning the loss of loved ones.
>
>Mourning themselves,
>
>>>>soon to be slaves.

>And the Greeks?
>
>>Exhausted from battle,
>>
>>>>starving,
>>
>>>all night scavenging what little they can find,
>>
>>they eat their scraps and
>>
>>sleep an untroubled sleep,
>>
>>>free of frost for once and an open sky,

in houses their spears captured,
                sleep unguarded and rise refreshed
                        like men blessed by the gods.

But the gods,
                the city's gods,
        the gods of the vanquished city,
                        what of them?

If tomorrow the conquering Greeks
        honor those gods,
                their altars,
        their temples and shrines,
                they themselves will not be conquered.
But let them —
                and this I fear gravely —
        let them succumb to greed and avarice,
        let them lust for spoils
                and blaspheme against the gods,
        and their homeward lap will be troubled.
But even if they appease the gods
                and come safely home,
        the agony of the dead may be wakened
                and demand payment;
                        and if not that,
        then some unexpected calamity.

                        So.
This is my tale, my fable, as you say.
                A woman's words.
                Nothing more.
But let good prevail for all to see.
And let it end here,

the murders, the evils.
We have much to hope for.
And I have much hope.

FIRST OLD MAN:
Spoken wisely and like a man, to be sure.
Armed with such "proofs" and "certainty,"
let us now give thanks to the gods,
for the joy we feel is worth all the pain suffered.

****

from **AGAMEMNON** (458 BCE)

[Agamemnon is now dead, and the debate on the justice of the murder comes forward. Clytemnestra attempts to justify herself. The First Old Man presents another view. Psychology, culture, and ethics are powerfully displayed. A burden of judgment lies on the playgoer, as Aeschylus intended.]

CHARACTERS

Clytemnestra (Klytaimnêstra)
First Old Man

(The central doors open and enter SLAVES with the corpses of AGAMEMNON and KASSANDRA which they toss to the ground. KLYTAIMNÊSTRA enters close behind and stands triumphantly above them with bloodied sword.)

KLYTAIMNÊSTRA:
Words.

        Many.

Many, many words have I
      spoken, words to suit the
   moment, cautious
      words, but here's an
          end,
an end without
   shame.

I've paid my debt.
Blood with blood.
Hate with hate.
    How else could I have
      strung my nets of doom high enough

to prevent overleaping? How else
have trapped an enemy who pretended loving
                              friendship?
And now it's done.
And I have won.
And I stand here where I struck to end the agony
     of my long planning, this ancient
          curse, years-long in the fermenting,
               and he never knew,
     there was no escape, no way
          to ward off death. And I deny
               none of it,
                    none.

I catch him then like a fish,
     in a mesh of rich
          webbing, and I strike, I
               strike, strike twice,
                    twice, once,
     then again,
          again, and he cries twice,
               twice to the heavens, and then he's
     limp, his legs give way, his
          tendons slacken, and he
          falls,
     down,
          down into the crimson swirl,
               and then another, another
          strike, a third, three
               blows, the last for Zeus beneath the earth,
     Zeus Keeper of Corpses, a third
               strike to keep the ritual proper.

He falls, his huge body,
    and a sharp jet of blood spurting,
    falling on me, spattering, like a
dark shower of crimson
    dew, and I revel in it,
        revel like a field of
flowers revels in spring in the sweet rain
                of Zeus' heaven.

I rest my case, noble gentlemen of Argos.
    Rejoice if it's your will;
        as for me,
    I exult in my triumph.

If I had poured the libation this corpse deserves,
    no wine could have matched the
        deserving curse of my words.
He filled every bowl in this house
        with a multitude of evil,
and now comes home to drain it to the
              dregs.

FIRST OLD MAN:
    I'm stunned with disbelief, woman,
    at your arrogance — over the body
    of the husband you've just murdered.

KLYTAIMNÊSTRA:
    Don't treat me like some witless girl.
    I'm not on trial here.
    Praise or blame me,
        it's all one to me.
    This is Agamemnon.
        And this is my husband.
            And that husband is now a corpse.

The work of this right hand that killed him justly.

(Music. Song. Dance.)

FIRST OLD MAN: *(Sings.)*
What root from the earth,
what drug from the sea have you taken
to make you do such a thing?
You murdered your husband.
The people curse you for your deed.
You cut him down, you cast him away,
and now you, too, will be cast away,
an exile, condemned,
thrown from the city,
an object of hatred and revulsion.

(SCENE CONTINUES)

****

from **LIBATION BEARERS** (458 BCE)

[Electra and Orestes, the children of Agamemnon and Clytemnestra, meet at their father's grave and reveal their need to avenge his murder and also the moral difficulty of killing their mother. The choice is bitter and passion filled. Daughter and son have their own distinctive ways of confronting the dilemma.]

CHARACTERS

>Electra (Êlektra)
>First Libation Bearer
>Orestes (Orestês)
>Chorus of Libation Bearers

>*(Outside Agamemnon's Palace. Agamemnon's tomb and grave mound downstage.)*

ÊLEKTRA: *(Sings.)*
>Zeus!
>>Zeus!
>Give us our rights!
>Smash them,
>crush,
>break in their
>>>skulls!
>Kill!
>>Kill!
>Show us your power!
>Let the land
>believe once more.
>I demand
>justice from
>>>injustice.

Great Earth,
Great Mother,
hear me,
and hear me,
lords of the
			earth below!

FIRST LIBATION BEARER: *(Sings.)*

There is a law.
Blood will have blood.
Blood spilt
demands more
			blood.
Murder
shrieks in the
night,
Murder
calls for the
			Furies.
"Furies, come!
Aid the long dead!
Demand blood for blood!"
Ruin demands ruin!
Destruction, destruction!

ORESTÊS: *(Sings.)*

Lords of the underworld,
infernal gods,
			hear us!
O hear us,
			exalted
Curses of the dead!
Behold in us the
end of the race of
Atreus,

helpless,
dishonored,
despairing,
shamed,
with only bare
life to cling to,
adrift on a
shoreless sea.
Where can we
                    turn,
Great Zeus?
Where?

LIBATION BEARERS: *(Sing.)*

> To hear such grief, my king,
> makes me tremble with fear.
> My eyes turn inward,
> I see black despair.
> But when confidence wakens
> and hope stands firm,
> my heart's pain fades and
> hope appears in all her beauty.

ÊLEKTRA: *(Sings.)*

What must we do
to rouse you, brother?
Recite our
            agonies,
the pain we've
                suffered?
Let her fawn.
Let her try.
Let the wolf-mother
smile and smile!
She bore us,

she bore

      two wolves,

and we will

not be

softened,

not appeased

by the

      savage

she-wolf!

FIRST LIBATION BEARER: *(Sings.)*

Dead,

      o dead,

when he lay

      dead,

Agamemnon,

my head, my breast,

I beat them,

beat them,

like a Persian

      mourner,

my arms stretched high,

beat,

      beat down,

my hands clutched,

tearing hair, fists

pounding,

spattering blood,

blows

      resounding

on my battered and

wretched head.

ÊLEKTRA: *(Sings.)*

IOOO!

IOOO!
Cruel mother!
Reckless mother!
Evil wife!
You buried him,
buried,
but a savage
        farewell,
savage,
no eyes to
        weep,
no people to
        mourn,
no lamentation for the
slain warrior!

FIRST LIBATION BEARER: *(Sings.)*

Listen, son,
hear me,
        Orestês.
You must know this.
The she-wolf
who
    murdered also
mutilated.
Hands, feet,
ears,
manhood,
lopped away,
tied to his neck,
slung through the
        armpits!
A crime to make his
death

unbearable to you.
You know now your
father's
      suffering,
his grave
      dishonor.

ÊLEKTRA: *(Sings.)*
    You've heard how he
    died, what they
    did to his
        body.
    They did the same
    to my
      life.
    They shut me away,
    no funeral mourning for me.
    Locked me in a room
    deep in the
        house,
    like a rabid bitch
    chained in a kennel.
    Laughter died in me
    that day, and
    tears ran
      channels
    in my cheeks.
    A secret
      mourning,
    a private
      lament.
    You know now, brother,
    you know now,
      Orestês.

Carve it in your
heart
    forever.

LIBATION BEARERS: *(Sing.)*

                    Hear her, Orestês!
            Let her words ring in your ears!
                  Remember.
              The past is past.
             The future is all!
       Raise up your heart now in rage
           and enter the battle!

ORESTÊS: *(Sings.)*

Your tale is a tale of
dishonor!
      His,
yours,
      the people!
My father's body,
naked,
mangled!
And her hands did it!
Dishonored his body,
dishonored his
         memory!
She'll pay!
By god she'll pay!
The gods are with us!
And my hands with them!
And when I have
        slain her,
I can die happy!

Come, father,

come,
join us in battle!

ÊLEKTRA: *(Sings.)*
Bathed in tears, I call on you, father!

FIRST LIBATION BEARER: *(Sings.)*
Together,
as one,
in a single
cry,
we call to you,
Master,
to come to the
light!
Join our battle
against the hated!

ORESTÊS: *(Sings.)*
Let force battle
force,
let Justice battle
Justice!

ÊLEKTRA: *(Sings.)*
Bring Retribution in a way that is just!

FIRST LIBATION BEARER: *(Sings.)*
I shudder to hear
these
prayers.
The hour of doom has
long been waiting.
And prayer will
surely bring it.

LIBATION BEARERS: *(Sing.)*

> Deadly curse bred in the race,
> evil, bloody, discordant stroke,
> the rage of Ruin,
> unspeakable grief,
> unending pain!

> There is no cure but one;
> no outside hand can set it right,
> only the children,
> only their hands.
> Strife,
> savage, brutal strife.
> The only cure: blood for blood.
> To the gods below we sing this hymn!

> Hear us, blest Powers beneath the earth!
> Give us your aid,
> send us help!
> Bless these children!
> Give them victory!

(Music out.)

ORESTÊS:

Father, who died an unkingly death,
answer my prayer:
> give me your throne.

ÊLEKTRA:

I ask, too, father: let me escape
when I have brought ruin
> down on Aigisthos.

ORESTÊS:

For then when men feast the dead
you will get your share of honor.
If not, and I fail,
you will lose both feast and honor.

ÊLEKTRA:

And on my wedding day I will bring you
the best my father's house has to offer.
But first, father,
I will honor this tomb.

ORESTÊS:

Earth, send up my father to witness my battle.

ÊLEKTRA:

Persephonê, Queen of the Underworld, give him victory.

ORESTÊS:

Remember the bath, father, that robbed you of life.

ÊLEKTRA:

Remember the net they fashioned to catch you up.

ORESTÊS:

The fetters that caught you up were made in no smithy.

ÊLEKTRA:

They plotted to trap you in a web of shame.

ORESTÊS:

Father, how can you sleep through these taunts?

ÊLEKTRA:

Lift your head, come up to us, father.

ORESTÊS:

Either send Justice to fight on our side,
the side of those you love and
who love you, or let us kill them

by their own means,
        grip for grip,
        cunning for cunning.
They threw you, won't you help
            us throw them?

ÊLEKTRA:

This is our last cry to you, father,
        your eagle's brood,
        your fledglings,
            here at your tomb.

Pity us,
            Orestês,
                Êlektra,
        pity your children.

ORESTÊS:

Don't blot out the race of Pelops.
While we live, you live,
            even in death.

ÊLEKTRA:

Listen, father, it's for your sake we do this.
        Honor our prayer.
            Save your name.

FIRST LIBATION BEARER:

Your words are without
        fault, my dears. They have never
mourned with libations this
        tomb or his fate.
But now you're set,
        your minds made up,
        only the act awaits you.
The time is come.
        Do the deed.
            Test your fortune.

ORESTÊS:

And we will.

But first a question.

Why has she sent these libations

now, after so long, after

years,

and too late?

What was she thinking?

A futile gift to heal a wound past curing,

to a man who's dead and hates her?

What sense does it make? And so

paltry an offering as that? A mockery

to the enormity of her offence! No act,

however great, can ever atone

for the taking of a life.

Why did she do this? Why?

What's her reason?

FIRST LIBATION BEARER:

I can tell you that, son.

I was there.

Dreams.

Terrible dreams.

Roaming the night.

Haunting her. Making her wander,

distracted, in unspeakable

fear.

And so she sent these

gifts, these libations —

the godless woman.

ORESTÊS:

What was this dream? Tell me.

FIRST LIBATION BEARER:

She dreamt she gave birth to a snake.

ORESTÊS:

And?

FIRST LIBATION BEARER:

She wrapped it. In swaddling clothes. Like a child.

ORESTÊS:

Did this monster cry for food?

FIRST LIBATION BEARER:

She fed it at her breast.

ORESTÊS:

Surely it didn't bite her?

FIRST LIBATION BEARER:

No, but it sucked a clot of blood in the milk.

ORESTÊS:

This is no empty dream. This was a man.

FIRST LIBATION BEARER:

She screamed out in her sleep in terror
    and ran wildly through the house.
Lamps were lighted everywhere
    till the palace glowed with light.
        She then sent these. Libations,
    funeral libations. And us to bring them
    to the dead to make a cure and
        end her distress.

ORESTÊS:

I pray to Earth, and the infernal Powers below,
    and to you spirits that summon up
    dreams to men, and my father's
            tomb!

Let this dream be made flesh in me!
        This is all of a piece.
I see it now. Born from the same place
    I was born, wrapped in the same
    cloths I was wrapped in, fed by the same
    breast that fed me, and drew from that breast
    milk with clots of
        blood; and then she shrieks out in
            terror — what can it be,
    that the horrendous portent,
but that the woman who nursed a monstrous
        vision, must also die a
    monstrous death!
        I am that snake.
        My sword is my sting.
        The dream is true.

                        ****

from **EUMENIDES** (458 BCE)

[The priestess Pythia begins her day of prophecy at the temple of
Apollo in Delphi. She praises many of the high gods, especially for their
role in civilizing Athens. Then she enters the temple and recoils in horror at the uncivilized consequences of the murders of Agamemnon
and Clytemnestra. How is the project of civilization to be continued?
Aeschylus proposes a solution in the *Eumenides*, but perhaps we have
even now not become civilized enough. Perhaps that is a reason why we
still read Aeschylus.]

CHARACTER

Pythia

*(Sunrise. Delphi. The sanctuary of Pythian Apollo. PYTHIA, dressed in
white, stands at the central door.)*

PYTHIA:

To Mother Earth
I give pride of place in my prayer,
Gaia,
prophet,
first of gods;
then to Themis, her daughter,
protector of Law and
Tradition, the second, as legend
tells, to hold her mother's
prophetic seat;
and third in line is Phoibê,
Bright One, Titaness and
daughter of Earth,
a seat given in peace and
calm.
And she in turn gave it, a birthday

gift, to Apollo, along with her
　　name:
Phoibos Apollo he is,
　　god of prophecy and light.

Leaving the lake and rocky ridge of
　　Dêlos, he came to Athêna's ship-thronged
　　shores, and then to this
　　　　land, and took his prophetic
　　seat here on
　　　　　　Parnassos.
His escort? The sons of Hephaistos,
　　god of fire, road-builders,
men of Athens, who tamed the
　　wilds and civilized our savage
　　　　　　country.

And the people honored him,
　　　　Apollo,
　　lining the roads on his way, and
Delphos, our king and
　　steersman of our state, praised him
　　　　greatly, and Zeus breathed
inspiration into his mind, the art of
　　divination, and set him,
　　　　his son,
fourth in line of
　　prophets, here on this
　　　　throne, he who sees, and
　　he who speaks.
And it is for Zeus he
　　speaks; for none but
　　　　Father Zeus.

These gods I honor first in my prayers.
                But Athêna of the
     Precinct I honor
        most. And I revere the
Nymphs in the Korykan Cavern,
       the haunt of wheeling birds and
          gods. And Bromios, too,
Dionysos, Roaring God, and
       not to be forgotten, rules here, too.
Dionysos who, at the head of his
       army of Bakkhai, hunted down
       Pentheus, netting him like a
          hare in flight and ripping him
       in pieces.

I honor also the sweet waters of
       Pleistos, and Poseidon I honor,
         mighty Poseidon, and
Zeus Fulfiller,
Zeus Most High.

I will now take my seat on the
       throne as prophet, and pray the gods
       for a consultation far better than
          any before.

If any Greeks are present,
       they may enter, as custom
       allows, in the order chosen by
         lot, for my prophecy comes
whatever way the god leads me.

(Exit PYTHIA into the temple by the central door. After a silence her screams of terror are heard from inside, and a moment later she emerges crawling on all fours in a state of hysteria.)

Horror!

Horror!

Horror for any eyes, what I saw!

Horrible!

Too weak to stand with my
    fright! I scramble on
        hands and knees! A feeble old
    woman — a nothing — a babbling
        baby with what I've
                    seen!

Foul!

Foul!

In the temple — there in the
    temple — there —

(She rises slowly to her feet.)

On my way to the inner shrine,
    garlanded everywhere with
        green wreaths, there at the
Navelstone, I saw him,
        a man, horrible sight,
                horrible,
    polluted, an abomination to the
        gods, there, sitting where
suppliants sit, hands
    bloody, bloody
        sword drawn, dripping,
    bloody, and a tall branch of
            olive twined with bright
    wool, a silvery
    fleece.

And around him,
    everywhere, sprawled on stone
    benches, asleep, a ghastly

crew of women — women? — no,
women they are not, not
women,
Gorgons — but no, not even Gorgons.

I saw once in a painting the
figures of creatures that
carried off the feast of Phineus.
But these have no wings,
all black, loathsome,
hateful. When they
breathe they snort, and their
mouths and noses drip and
bubble, too terrible to
approach.
Their eyes,
ulcerated,
run with blood and pus.
Unclean!
Abominable sight!
Unfit for the statues of gods or
human dwelling!
Where they are from I don't know.
What country could have bred them and not
regretted their evil error?
But this must be mighty Apollo's concern.
Apollo seer, Apollo great
healer.
Apollo, Apollo, come, purify your
halls!

(Exit PYTHIA.)

****

from **PROMETHEUS BOUND** (456 BCE)

[Prometheus is chained to a rock, and as every day begins, he is torn apart by birds only to be made whole again at night. Prometheus laments for his endless suffering for defying Zeus by giving fire to humans. Yet the lament is defiance, born of freedom and defiance of tyranny.]

CHARACTER

Prometheus (Promêtheus)

(Skythia. A desolate mountain crag at the edge of the world.)

PROMÊTHEUS: *(Speaks.)*
 O Light,
  Light,
   blessèd Light,
  bright Light of
  day, gleaming sky,
 swift-winged winds, and
  rivers, springing, fed by
   Ocean, countless, uncountable
 laughing ocean waves, and
  Earth, our mother, mother of us
   all, and Sun, great
  Sun that sees over all,
   all-seeing round,
 I call on you to see what a god may
  suffer at the hands of gods!

(Chants.)

Here is my agony,
here is my torment,

these I will battle
through ten thousand years.
Here,
here is the torture
the new Tyrant of the Blest
has made for me,
bondage,
shameful,
unspeakable!
AIIII!
AIIII!
I groan in pain present,
and groan for pain to be!
When will it end?
Where has he set
the limit?
Where?

(Speaks.)

But what am I saying?
     I know the future.
          I know what will come.
Forethought they named me, the gods.
No pain will be unexpected,
     and it will come. I'll bear it,
          my fate, as best I can,
     for I know one thing for certain:
Necessity cannot be wrestled down.
     To speak, not to speak,
     both are hard, for both I am
                         punished.
I gave our privilege,
     the gods' great privilege,

to man, to mortals, and for
that I am yoked to
                    Necessity,
        to this.
From the secret stores of
        heaven I searched out fire,
                the fount of fire,
                where it begins, its
        source, and stashed it, a spark,
in a fennel stalk, and gave it to
                    man:
fire that gives every skill,
        every craft, every art,
        fire that fulfils every
need.
This is my crime, and for this
        I am punished, for this I
                pay, naked, nailed to this
        rock, staked, chained beneath this
                enormity of sky.

(A distant rushing sound as if of wings approaches.)
(Sings.)

Á! Á!
        ÉA! ÉA!
What? What
                sound,
what smell, what
perfume floats by me
on the
        air?
I can't see it,
what it is!

Divine?

  Human?

A demigod?

   What?

What comes to this

rock at the world's

    edge

to see my

  sufferings?

(Chants.)

Behold me,

here,

you I cannot see,

I, a god,

a prisoner chained,

an enemy of Zeus and

all who throng his palace halls!

I who loved man

too much!

This rustle of wings!

I hear it again!

Near!

Nearer!

Wings of birds?

The air whispers

with wings!

I'm afraid!

       ****

Aeschylus

THE READING ROOM

YOUNG ACTORS AND THEIR TEACHERS

Aeschylus. *Complete Plays: Four Plays*. Vol. II. Translated by Carl R. Mueller. Hanover, N.H.: Smith and Kraus, 2002.

_____. *Complete Plays: Oresteia*. Vol. I. Translated by Carl R. Mueller. Hanover, N.H.: Smith and Kraus, 2002.

Bieber, Margarete. *The History of the Greek and Roman Theater*. 2nd ed. Revised. Princeton, N.J.: Princeton University Press, 1961.

Burkert, Walter. *Greek Religion*. Cambridge, Mass.: Harvard University Press, 1985.

Finley, M. I. *The Ancient Greeks: An Introduction to Their Life and Thought*. New York: The Viking Press, 1964.

Green, J. R. *Theatre in Ancient Greek Society*. London and New York: Routledge, 1994.

Guthrie, W. K. C. *The Greeks and Their Gods*. London: Methuen, 1950.

Ley, Graham. *A Short Introduction to the Ancient Greek Theater*. Chicago: The University of Chicago Press, 1991.

Rehm, Rush. *The Greek Tragic Theatre*. London and New York: Routledge, 1992.

Segal, Erich. *Oxford Essays in Greek Tragedy*. Oxford: Oxford University Press, 1984.

Traulos, Johannes. *Pictorial Dictionary of Ancient Athens*. London: Thames and Hudson, 1971.

Vickers, Brian. *Towards Greek Tragedy*. London: Longman, 1973.

Walcot, Peter. *Greek Drama in Its Theatrical and Social Context*. Cardiff: The University of Wales Press, 1976.

This extensive bibliography lists books about the playwright according to whom the books might be of interest. If you would like to research further something that interests you in the text, lists of references, sources cited, and editions used in this book are found in this section.

Winkler, John J., and Froma I. Zeitlin, eds. *Nothing to Do with Dionysos? Athenian Drama in Its Social Context.* Princeton, N.J.: Princeton University Press, 1992.

Winnington-Ingram, R. P. *Studies in Aeschylus.* Cambridge: Cambridge University Press, 1983.

SCHOLARS, STUDENTS, PROFESSORS

Adkins, A. W. H. *Merit and Responsibility: A Study in Greek Values.* Oxford: Oxford University Press, 1960.

Aylen, Leo. *The Greek Theater.* Rutherford, N.J.: Fairleigh Dickinson University Press, 1985.

Barker, Ernest. *The Politics of Aristotle.* Oxford: Oxford University Press, 1946.

Bennett, Simon, M. D. *Mind and Madness in Ancient Greece.* Ithaca, N.Y.: Cornell University Press, 1978.

Blundell, Sue. *Women in Ancient Greece.* London: British Museum Press, 1995.

Boesche, Roger. *The Theories of Tyranny from Plato to Arendt.* University Park: The Pennsylvania State University Press, 1996.

Bury, J. B., and Russell Meiggs. *A History of Greece to the Death of Alexander the Great.* 4th ed. Revised. New York: St. Martin's Press, 1991.

Buxton, R. G. *Persuasion in Greek Tragedy.* Cambridge: Cambridge University Press, 1982.

Cameron, H. D. *Studies on the Seven Against Thebes of Aeschylus.* The Hague: Mouton, 1971.

Conacher, D. J. *Aeschylus' Prometheus Bound: A Literary Commentary.* Toronto and London: The University of Toronto Press, 1980.

_____. *Aeschylus' Oresteia: A Literary Commentary.* Toronto: University of Toronto Press, 1987.

Cooper, Lane. *The Greek Genius and Its Influence.* New Haven, Conn.: Yale University Press, 1917.

Csapo, Eric, and William J. Slater. *The Context of Ancient Drama.* Ann Arbor: The University of Michigan Press, 1995.

Dodds, E. R. *The Greeks and the Irrational.* Berkeley and Los Angeles: University of California Press, 1951.

Fergusson, Francis. *The Idea of Theater: A Study of Ten Plays, The Art of Drama in Changing Perspective*. Princeton, N.J.: Princeton University Press; London: Oxford University Press, 1949.

Forrest, W. G. *The Emergence of Greek Democracy*. New York: McGraw-Hill, 1966.

Gagarin, M. *Aeschylean Drama*. Berkeley and Los Angeles: The University of California Press, 1976.

Garkand, Robert. *The Greek Way of Life*. Ithaca, N.Y.: Cornell University Press, 1990.

Georgiades, Thrasybulos. *Greek Music, Verse and Dance*. New York: Da Capo Press, 1973.

Gombrich, Ernst. *Art and Illusion*. London: Phaidon, 1977.

Green, J. R., and E. Handley. *Images of the Greek Theatre*. Austin: University of Texas Press, 1995

Griffith, M. *Aeschylus: Prometheus Bound*. Cambridge: Cambridge University Press, 1983.

Hall, Edith. *Inventing the Barbarian: Greek Self-definition through Tragedy*. Oxford: Oxford University Press, 1989.

_____. *Aeschylus: Persians*. Warminster, UK: Aris and Phillips, 1996.

Halperin, David M. *One Hundred Years of Homosexuality*. New York and London: Routledge, 1990.

Herington, C. J. *Poetry into Drama: Early Tragedy and the Greek Poetic Tradition*. Berkeley and Los Angeles: The University of California Press, 1985.

_____. *Aeschylus*. New Haven, Conn.: Yale University Press, 1986.

Hogan, James C. *Commentary on the Complete Greek Tragedies: Aeschylus*. Chicago: The University of Chicago Press, 1984.

Hornblower, Simon, and Antony Spawforth, eds. *The Oxford Classical Dictionary*. 3rd ed. Oxford: Oxford University Press, 1996.

Jones, John. *On Aristotle and Greek Tragedy*. Stanford, Calif.: Stanford University Press, 1980.

Jung, Carl Gustav, and Carl Kerényi. *Essays on a Science of Mythology: The Myth of the Divine Child and the Mysteries of Eleusis*. Bollingen Series XXII. Princeton. N.J.: Princeton University Press, 1969.

Just, Roger. *Women in Athenian Law and Life*. London and New York: Routledge, 1991.

Kerényi, Carl. *Poiesis: Structure and Thought*. Berkeley and Los Angeles: The University of California Press, 1966.

_____. *Form and Meaning in Drama: A Study of Six Greek Plays and of Hamlet*. 2nd ed. London: Methuen, 1964; New York: Barnes and Noble, 1968.

_____. *Dionysos: Archetypal Image of Indestructible Life*. Princeton and London: Princeton University Press, 1976.

_____. *Word and Action: Essays on the Ancient Theater*. Baltimore and London: The Johns Hopkins University Press, 1979.

Keuls, Eva C. *The Reign of the Phallus: Sexual Politics in Ancient Athens*. Berkeley and Los Angeles: The University of California Press, 1993.

Knox, Bernard M. *The Heroic Temper*. Berkeley: The University of California Press, 1964.

_____. *Word and Action: Essays on the Ancient Theater*. Baltimore, Md.: The Johns Hopkins University Press, 1979.

Kolb, Frank. *Agora und Theater*. Berlin: Gebrüder Mann, 1981.

Kott, Jan. *The Eating of the Gods: An Interpretation of Greek Tragedy*. New York: Random House, 1973.

Kuhns, Richard F. *The House, the City and the Judge: The Growth of Moral Awareness in the Oresteia*. Indianapolis: Bobbs-Merrill, 1962.

Lax, Batya Casper. *Elektra: A Gender Sensitive Study of the Plays Based on the Myth*. North Carolina and London: McFarland and Company, Inc, 1995.

Lloyd-Jones, Hugh. *The Justice of Zeus*. Sather Gate Lectures, Vol. 41. Berkeley and Los Angeles: The University of California Press, 1971.

Lonsdale, Stephen H. *Dance and Ritual Play in Greek Religion*. Baltimore, Md.: The Johns Hopkins University Press, 1993.

Macleod, C. W. "Clothing in the *Oresteia*." *Maia*, 25, 1973.

Mastronarde, D. *Contact and Disunity: Some Conventions of Speech and Action on the Greek Tragic Stage*. Berkeley and Los Angeles: The University of California Press, 1979.

Meier, Christian. *The Greek Discovery of Politics*. Cambridge: Harvard University Press, 1993.

_____. *The Political Art of Greek Tragedy*. Baltimore, Md.: The Johns Hopkins University Press, 1993.

Neils, Jenifer. *Goddess and Polis: The Panathenaic Festival in Ancient Athens*. Princeton, N.J.: Princeton University Press, 1992.

Neuberg, M. *An Aeschylean Universe*. Ann Arbor: The University of Michigan Press, 1981.

Neumann, Erich. *The Great Mother: An Analysis of the Archetype*. 2nd ed. Bollingen Series XLVII. New York: Pantheon Books, 1963.

_____. *The Origins and History of Consciousness*. 2nd printing, corrected and amended. Bollingen Series XVII. New York: Pantheon Books, 1964.

Nietzsche, Friedrich. *The Birth of Tragedy and Other Writings*. Cambridge Texts in the History of Philosophy. Cambridge: Cambridge University Press, 1999.

Otto, Walter. *Dionysus, Myth and Cult*. Bloomington: University of Indiana Press, 1965.

Parke, H. W. *Festivals of the Athenians*. Ithaca, N.Y.: Cornell University Press, 1977.

Pickard-Cambridge, A. W. *The Theatre of Dionysus in Athens*. Oxford: The Clarendon Press, 1968.

_____. *Dithyramb, Tragedy and Comedy*. 2nd ed. Revised by T. B. L. Webster. Oxford: Oxford University Press, 1988.

_____. *The Dramatic Festivals of Athens*. 2nd ed. Revised by John Gould and D. M. Lewis. Oxford: The Clarendon Press, 1988.

Podlecki, Anthony J. *The Political Background of Aeschylean Tragedy*. Ann Arbor: The University of Michigan Press, 1966.

Pomeroy, S. *Goddesses, Whores, Wives, and Slaves: Women in Classical Antiquity*. New York: Shocken, 1995.

Prag, A. J. N. *The Oresteia: Iconographic and Narrative Tradition*. Warminster, UK: Aris and Phillips, 1985.

Reinhardt, Karl. *Aischylos als Regisseur und Theologe*. Bern: A. Franke, 1949.

Rosenmeyer, Thomas. G. *The Masks of Tragedy*. Austin: The University of Texas, 1963.

Seaford, Richard. *Reciprocity and Ritual: Homer and Tragedy in the Developing City State*. Oxford: Oxford University Press, 1994.

Segal, Charles. *Interpreting Greek Tragedy: Myth, Poetry, Text*. Ithaca, N.Y.: Cornell University Press, 1986.

Slater, Philip. *The Glory of Hera*. Boston: Beacon Press, 1968.

Smyth, Herbert Weir. *Aeschylus*. 2 vols. Cambridge: Harvard University Press, 1963.

Sourvinou-Inwood, Christine. *Reading Greek Culture: Texts and Images, Rituals and Myths*. Oxford: Oxford University Press, 1991.

Steiner, George. *The Death of Tragedy*. New York: Alfred A. Knopf, 1961.

Thomson, George. *Aeschylus and Athens*. London: Lawrence and Wishart, 1973.

Turner, Victor. *The Forest of Symbols*. Ithaca, N.Y.: Cornell University Press, 1973.

_____. *Dramas, Fields, and Metaphors*. Ithaca, N,Y,: Cornell University Press, 1974.

Vernant, Jean-Pierre. *Myth and Thought Among the Greeks*. London and Boston: Routledge and Kegan Paul, 1983.

_____. *Myth and Society in Ancient Greece*. New York: Zone Books, 1990.

Vernant, Jean-Pierre, and Pierre Vidal-Naquet, eds. *Myth and Tragedy in Ancient Greece*. New York: Zone Books, 1990.

Winkler, John. *The Constraints of Desire: The Anthropology of Sex and Gender in Ancient Greece*. New York and London: Routledge, 1990.

Zeitlin, Froma I. *Under the Sign of the Shield: Semiotics and Aeschylus' Seven Against Thebes*. Rome: Edizioni dell'Atenes, 1982.

_____. *Playing the Other: Gender and Society in Classical Greek Literature*. Chicago: University of Chicago Press, 1996.

THEATER, PRODUCERS

Bartsch, S. *Actors in the Audience*. Cambridge: Harvard University Press, 1994.

Else, Gerald F. *The Origin and Early Form of Greek Tragedy*. Martin Classical Lectures, Vol. 20. Cambridge: Harvard University Press, 1965.

Flickinger, R. C. *The Greek Theater and Its Drama*. Chicago: University of Chicago Press, 1936.

_____. *Aeschylus: The Creator of Tragedy*. Oxford: Oxford University Press, 1940.

Murray, Gilbert. *Five Stages of Greek Religion*. New York: Columbia University Press, 1925.

Page, Denys L. *Actors' Interpolations in Greek Tragedy*. Oxford: The Clarendon Press, 1934.

Roberts, Patrick. *The Psychology of Tragic Drama*. Boston and London: Routledge and Kegan Paul, 1975.

Sutton, D. F. *The Greek Satyr Play*. Meisenheim am Glan: Hain, 1980.

Wiles, David. *Tragedy in Athens*. Cambridge and New York: Cambridge University Press, 1997.

ACTORS, DIRECTORS, THEATER PROFESSIONALS

Aristotle. *The Poetics*. Translated by Gerald Else. Ann Arbor: University of Michigan Press, 1967.

Arnott, Peter. *Greek Scenic Conventions in the Fifth Century B.C.* Oxford: Oxford University Press, 1962.

_____. *Public and Performance in the Greek Theatre*. London: Routledge, 1989.

Bain, David. *Actors and Audience: A Study of Asides and Related Conventions in Greek Drama*. Oxford: Oxford University Press, 1977.

Bowen, A. *Aeschylus: Libation Bearers*. Bristol: Bristol Classical, 1986.

Broadhead, H. D. *Aeschylus: Persians*. Cambridge: Cambridge University Press, 1960.

Dale, A. M. *Collected Papers*. Cambridge: Cambridge University Press, 1969.

Denniston, J. D., and Denys L. Page. *Aeschylus: Agamemnon*. Oxford: Oxford University Press, 1957.

Detienne, Marcel. *Dionysus at Large*. Cambridge: Harvard University Press, 1989.

Fraenkel, E. *Aeschylus: Agamemnon*. 3 vols. Oxford: Oxford University Press, 1950.

Friis, Johansen H., and E. W. Whittle. *Aeschylus: Suppliant Women*. Copenhagen: Gyldendal, 1980

Garvie, A. F. *Aeschylus' Supplices: Play and Trilogy*. Cambridge: Cambridge University Press, 1969.

_____. *Language, Sexuality, Narrative: The Oresteia*. Cambridge: Cambridge University Press, 1984.

_____. *Aeschylus: Libation-Bearers*. Oxford: Oxford University Press, 1986.

Goldhill, Simon. *Reading Greek Tragedy*. Cambridge: Cambridge University Press, 1986.

_____. *Aeschylus: The Oresteia*. Cambridge: Cambridge University Press, 1992.

Hornby, Richard. *Script into Performance*. Austin: University of Texas Press, 1977.

Hutchinson, G. O. *Aeschylus: Seven Against Thebes*. Oxford: Oxford University Press, 1985.

Lattimore, Richmond. *The Poetry of Greek Tragedy*. Baltimore, Md.: The Johns Hopkins University Press, 1958.

_____. *The Story Patterns in Greek Tragedy*. Ann Arbor: The University of Michigan Press, 1964.

Lebeck, A. *The Oresteia*. Washington, D.C.: Center for Hellenic Studies, 1971.

Lesky, Albin. *Greek Tragedy*. London: Ernest Benn, 1978.

Michelini, Ann Norris. *Tradition and Dramatic Form in the Persians of Aeschylus*. Leiden: Brill, 1982.

Podlecki, Anthony. *Aeschylus: Eumenides*. Warminster, UK: Aris and Phillips, 1992.

Scott, William C. *Musical Design in Aeschylean Theatre*. Hanover: The University Press of New England, 1984.

Sommerstein, A. H. *Aeschylus. Eumenides*. Cambridge: Cambridge University Press, 1989.

Taplin, Oliver. *The Stagecraft of Aeschylus*. Oxford: The Clarendon Press, 1977.

_____. *Greek Tragedy in Action*. Berkeley and Los Angeles: The University of California Press; London: Methuen, 1978.

_____. *Comic Angels and Other Approaches to Greek Drama Through Vase-Paintings*. Oxford: Oxford University Press, 1993.

Thalmann, W. *Dramatic Art in Aeschylus' Seven Against Thebes*. New Haven, Conn.: Yale University Press, 1978.

Walton, J. Michael. *Greek Theatre Practice*. Westport and London: Greenwood Press, 1980.

_____. *The Greek Sense of Theatre: Tragedy Reviewed*. London and New York: Methuen, 1984.

THE EDITIONS OF AESCHYLUS' WORKS USED FOR THIS BOOK

Aeschylus. *The Complete Plays.* Vol. I: *Oresteia.* Translated by Carl R. Mueller. Lyme, N.H.: Smith and Kraus, 2002.

Aeschylus. *The Complete Plays.* Vol. II: *Four Plays.* Translated by Carl R. Mueller. Lyme, N.H.: Smith and Kraus, 2002.

SOURCES CITED IN THIS BOOK

Easterling, P. E., ed. *The Cambridge Companion to Greek Tragedy.* Cambridge: Cambridge University Press, 1997.

Ewans, Michael. *Aeschylean Inevitability: A Study of the Oresteia.* Ann Arbor: University of Michigan Press, 1971.

_____. *Wagner and Aeschylus: The Ring and the Oresteia.* New York: Cambridge University Press, 1982.

Jaeger, Werner. *Paideia: The Ideals of Greek Culture.* New York: Oxford University Press, 1945.

Kitto, H. D. F. *Greek Tragedy: A Literary Study.* 2nd ed. New York: Doubleday, 1964; 3rd ed. London: Methuen, 1966.

Thucydides. *The Peloponnesian Wars.* Translated by Rex Warner. Harmondsworth, UK: Penguin Classics, 1972.

Awards

"And the winner is . . . "

YEAR BCE	DIONYSIA FESTIVAL IN ATHENS	LENAEA FESTIVAL IN ATHENS
ca 534	Thespis *Unknown title*	
484	**Aeschylus** **Unknown title**	
476	Phrynichus *Phoenissae*	
468	Sophocles *Triptolemus*	
ca 467	**Aeschylus** **Seven Against Thebes**	
ca 463	**Aeschylus** **Danaid trilogy**	
ca 459	**Aeschylus** **Suppliant Women**	
ca 458	**Aeschylus** **Oresteia**	
455	Euripides *Daughters of Pelias* (third prize)	
447	Sophocles *Unknown title*	
442	A prize is institutionalized and first awarded to the best comic actor at the City Dionysia. (unknown recipient)	
441	Euripides *Unknown title*	
ca 439	Sophocles *Unknown title* (first prize) Euripides *Alcestis* (second prize)	

Unknown title = play lost

First prize unless otherwise specified

Aristophanes won prizes in the comedy genre; the others won in the tragedy genre.

INDEX

Acropolis 4, 8, 32

Agamemnon 27, 28, 31

agora 4

Ajax 15

Apollo 28, 29,31, 32, 33, 38

archon 11

Areopagus 28, 32, 33

arete 19, 20, 21

Aristophanes 15

Aristotle 11, 20, 21, 36

Athena 8, 15, 32, 33

Athens 1, 2, 3, 4, 5, 6, 7, 8, 9, 10,
     11, 13, 15, 19, 27, 32, 33

Attica 1, 2, 10

aulos 10, 18

autocracy 3

Bacchae 13, 15

choregoi 11

choreography 7, 9, 13, 18

chorus 5, 6, 7, 9, 10, 11, 12, 13,
     17, 18, 19, 22, 23, 26, 27,
     28, 29, 30, 31, 33, 34, 35, 39

Cleisthenes 2

comedy 3, 11

cult 1, 2, 8, 12, 13, 14

Cyclops 33

Danaid tetralogy 3, 4

dance 5, 6, 7, 9, 12, 13, 15

death 1, 4, 14, 15, 17, 21, 24, 27,
     29, 30, 31, 34, 36

deme 2

Demeter 1, 8

democracy 2, 3, 27

Dionysus 4, 5, 7, 8, 9, 11, 12, 13,
     14, 15, 26, 38

dithyramb 9, 11

Eleusinian Mysteries 1

Eleusis 1

Epidaurus 5

escape 12, 14, 15, 22, 29, 37

Eumenides 32

Euphorion 4

Euripides 13, 33

fire 34

freedom 3, 21, 38

Furies 27, 28, 31, 32, 33

Gela 3

Great (or City) Dionysia 3, 11, 13,
     15

Herodotus 16

Hieron 3

Hippolytus 14, 15

Homer(ic) 15, 20, 21

hubris-ate 16, 17, 19

Iliad 15, 20

The entries in the index include highlights from the main In an Hour essay portion of the book.

Io 22, 23, 24, 34, 35, 38, 39

Libation Bearers 30
logion 5
love 21, 26, 27
Lycurgia 4
lyre 10, 18

Marathon 2, 4, 21, 27
mask 8, 12, 13, 15
music(al) 3, 10, 13, 18, 33
nature 12, 26

Nicomachean Ethics 20

Odyssey 15, 20
Oedipus at Colonus 9, 23
Old Men 9, 17, 18, 28, 30
orchesis 5
Oresteia 3, 4, 6, 7, 8, 27, 28, 33

Persephone 1
Persia(n) 2, 3, 9, 15, 16, 17, 1µ8,
    19, 27
Persians 3, 5, 9, 15, 16, 17, 19
phallus 14
Pisistratus 2
Plataea 3, 16, 17
pottery 13
Prometheus Bound 4, 34
proskenion 5

Rhetoric 36
Rural Dionysia 11

Sacred Precinct of Dionysus 4
Salamis 2, 3, 9, 15, 16, 19, 21, 27
sanctuary 5, 23, 32

satyr play 4, 11, 12, 13, 33
Seven Against Thebes 3, 5, 6, 9,
    19, 21, 38, 39
sex(ual(ly)) 12, 13, 14, 15, 22,
    24, 25, 26, 27, 29, 33
Sicily 3
skene 5
song 10, 15, 18, 32, 33
Sophocles 3, 9, 13, 23
Sparta 8
stoa 5
superplot 22
Suppliants 3, 5, 14, 19, 21, 22,
    23, 24, 26, 38
Syracuse 3

Theban tetralogy 4
Thebes 19
Thorikos 7
Trachones 7
tragedy 3, 4, 6, 8, 9, 10, 11, 12,
    13, 14, 15, 16, 18, 19, 21,
    27, 35, 38
tyrant 2, 35, 36, 39

The Vita 4

Women of Aitna 3

Zeus 22, 23, 24, 25, 27, 33, 34,
    35, 36, 37, 38, 39

ABOUT THE AUTHOR

Carl Mueller was a professor in the Department of Theater at the University of California, Los Angeles, from 1967 until his death in 2008. There he directed and taught theater history, criticism, dramatic literature, and playwriting. He was educated at Northwestern University, where he received a B.S. in English. After work in graduate English at the University of California, Berkeley, he received his M.A. in Playwriting at UCLA, where he also completed his Ph.D. in Theater History and Criticism. In 1960–1961 he was a Fulbright Scholar in Berlin.

A translator for more than forty years, he translated and published works by Büchner, Brecht, Wedekind, Hauptmann, Hofmannsthal, and Hebbel, to name a few. His published translation of von Horváth's *Tales from the Vienna Woods* was given its London West End premiere in July 1999. For Smith and Kraus he translated individual volumes of plays by Schnitzler, Strindberg, Pirandello, Kleist, and Wedekind. His translation of Goethe's *Faust Part One* and *Part Two* appeared in 2004. He also translated for Smith and Kraus *Sophokles: The Complete Plays* (2000), a two-volume *Aeschylus: The Complete Plays* (2002), and a four-volume *Euripides: The Complete Plays* (2005). His translations have been performed in every English-speaking country and have appeared on BBC-TV.

Smith and Kraus wishes to acknowledge Dr. Susan Ford Wiltshire, Professor of Classics, Emerita, Vanderbilt University. She was immensely helpful with the spellings of Greek names and places.

We thank Hugh Denard, whose enlightened permissions policy reflects an understanding that copyright law is intended to both protect the rights of creators of intellectual property as well as to encourage its use for the public good.

Know the playwright, love the play.

Open a new door to theater study, performance, and audience satisfaction with these Playwrights In an Hour titles.

ANCIENT GREEK

Aeschylus   Aristophanes   Euripides   Sophocles

RENAISSANCE

William Shakespeare

MODERN

Anton Chekhov   Noël Coward   Lorraine Hansberry
Henrik Ibsen   Arthur Miller   Molière   Eugene O'Neill
Arthur Schnitzler   George Bernard Shaw   August Strindberg
Frank Wedekind   Oscar Wilde   Thornton Wilder
Tennessee Williams

CONTEMPORARY

Edward Albee   Alan Ayckbourn   Samuel Beckett
Theresa Rebeck   Sarah Ruhl   Sam Shepard   Tom Stoppard
August Wilson

To purchase or for more information
visit our web site inanhourbooks.com